THE

CELTIC
FOOTBALL

MISCELLANY

This book is dedicated to a few friends.

To Jimmy Johnstone for his superb foreword; Billy Nolan, the world's most fanatical and loyal Celtic fan I have ever had the pleasure of knowing; Craig McAughtrie for his guidance; David Potter for all his help with the players' biographies; Jeff Healey for securing the foreword from Celtic's greatest ever player, Wee Jinky; David Ross for providing the ideas behind many of the book's entries; David and Joe Gilhooley for painstakingly proofreading my work; and to my publisher, Martin Corteel, for having the faith in me to see the project through.

And last, but certainly not least, to Paddy Crerand. Paddy, you're a gentleman in the eyes of all Bhoys and Red Devils.

Thanks for all of your help Bhoys.

Hail Hail!
John

This edition published in 2006

Copyright © Carlton Books Limited 2006

Carlton Books Limited
20 Mortimer Street
London W1T 3JW

A CIP catalogue record for this book is available from the British Library

ISBN 10: 1-84442-162-7
ISBN 13: 978-1-84442-162-6
Editor: Martin Corteel
Project art editor: Darren Jordan
Production: Lisa French

Printed in Great Britain

THE

CELTIC
FOOTBALL
MISCELLANY

JOHN WHITE

WITH A FOREWORD BY THE LATE GREAT
JIMMY JOHNSTONE

CARLTON
BOOKS

❧ ABBREVIATIONS ❧

EC	European Cup
ECWC	European Cup Winners Cup
FA	Football Association
FIFA	Federation of International Football Associations
ICFC/FC	Inter Cities Fairs Cup/Fairs Cup (*also* Football Club)
P/W/D/L/F/A	Played/Won/Drawn/Lost/(Goals)For/(Goals)Against
SFA	Scottish Football Association
SLC	Scottish League Cup
SPL	Scottish Premier League
UCL	UEFA Champions League
UEFA	Union of European Football Associations

🎉 FOREWORD 🎉

When John asked me to write the foreword to his Celtic Miscellany, I was delighted to do so. John very kindly donated £1 from every copy of his *Hoops Quiz Book* to the Motor Neurone Disease Association, a charity I am very much involved with.

My association with Celtic goes back to when I was just 13 years old. Kicking an old ball around the streets of Glasgow, I was offered a job as a ballboy at Parkhead. I seized my opportunity willingly and made my Celtic first-team debut in 1963, just before my 19th birthday. When I made my debut, the former Celtic player and captain, Jimmy McGrory, was in charge at Parkhead, but it was under the legendary Jock Stein that I played my best football for the Hoops before leaving the club in 1975.

The highlight of my Celtic career is, without doubt, our magnificent European Cup win over the mighty Inter Milan in Lisbon on Thursday, 25 May 1967. Goals from Tommy Gemmell and Stevie Chalmers placed our names in the history books as the first Scottish club, and the first British club, to lift Europe's premier trophy for clubs. And all achieved by 11 Scottish boys who were all born within 30 miles of Parkhead. Those boys I played alongside that night will live forever in my heart and dreams: Ronnie Simpson, Jim Craig, Billy McNeill, Tommy Gemmell, Bobby Murdoch, John Clark, Willie Wallace, Steve Chalmers, Bertie Auld and Bobby Lennox. And, of course, not forgetting the contribution made by others who helped get us to Lisbon: Willie O'Neill, Charlie Gallagher, Joe McBride, John Hughes, all the backroom staff and last but most certainly not least, the Big Man himself, Jock Stein.

John's book is jam-packed full of wonderful items of trivia; unusual Old Firm encounters are vividly brought back to memory; historical facts and figures covering Celtic's opponents and former legends jump out at you; European glory nights are relived; record results are recorded; the greatest number of club appearances/goals etc. are noted; stories about strange occurrences are peppered throughout the book and every Celtic manager, and so much more, is included.

This book is a must-buy book for all Celtic fans, regardless of age, because it is both informative and entertaining. John has spent a lot of time researching his material and it will both astound and please you in equal measure. I dare you to pick it up without reading it from front cover to last in one go, and then, if you're like me, you'll read it time and time again.

Jimmy Johnstone
January 2006

❧ ACKNOWLEDGEMENTS ☙

Special thanks to the webmaster at www.wikpedia.org for providing such an informative database on most football clubs around the world which helped me verify data and which also helped me obtain information on a number of subjects.

My thanks to David Ross and Forrest Robertson at www.scottishleague.net, which provides a comprehensive, and regularly updated, section on Scottish football.

My thanks to David Potter for his help with the players' biographies plus several other entries.

My thanks to Craig McAughtrie and John Dempster at www.keep-the-faith.net for all their assistance.

My thanks to Joe and David Gilhooley for taking the time to read through my work and to point out the occasional error.

And, last but by no means least, my thanks go to my wife Janice and our two sons, Marc and Paul, for their constant support.

❧ INTRODUCTION ❧

Think of Glasgow Celtic Football Club and the words *History, Pride, Passion, Glory* and *Religion* all come to mind.

However, had it not been for a certain Brother Walfrid, the team that just won their 13th League Cup and clinched their 40th league championship in season 2005–06 would not be the dominant force in Scottish football that it is today. The club was formally constituted in St Mary's Church Hall in East Rose Street (now Forbes Street), Calton, on 6 November 1887. Brother Walfrid's idea was to have a football club that would help alleviate poverty in Glasgow's East End parishes. Today, Glasgow is a thriving European city with Celtic one of the most financially viable clubs in European football.

Celtic is steeped in history from its formation up until the present day with the famous green and white hooped shirts known the world over. There have been many defining moments that have helped shape the history of the Bhoys, and in this book I hope to take you on a magical journey that will hopefully rekindle many wonderful moments, provide you with some unusual statistics, fascinating trivia, intriguing facts and figures about managers and players, plus many Cup, League and European glory day memories. However, my one hope, as you read this book, is that you scratch your head at least once and say, "I didn't know that." If I can make you do that, then all the hours I spent compiling the book will have been worthwhile.

Celtic have had many wonderful players throughout their illustrous history, and I am very proud to say that the man voted Celtic's Greatest Ever Player, Jimmy Johnstone, very kindly provided the Foreword for my book. Wee Jinky was a gentleman and football legend who simply lit up grounds, no matter where he played, and every time he had the ball, crowds just watched in awe at the Wee Man's brilliance. Jimmy had it all: mesmerizing dribbling skills, lightning fast pace, strength and the heart of a lion, a true Lisbon Lion. Jinky lost only one battle in life, his brave fight against Motor Neurone Disease because, sadly, he died on 13 March 2006. However, as a testimony to his genius, football fans all over Britain mourned his passing, with many Rangers fans paying their own heartfelt tributes to a true Scottish hero.

So, in closing, I hope my book will not only bring back memories of the Lisbon Lions' victory over Inter Milan in the European Cup Final on 25 May 1967, but also many other glory days when the players of Glasgow Celtic Football Club made you proud to be a Bhoy.

Hail, Hail!

John White
May 2006

🏴 WE ARE THE CHAMPIONS (1) 🏴

Celtic's first league championship success, at the third attempt, came in the 1892–93 season. Celtic had suffered disappointment in the two cups, losing in the final in both the Scottish Cup and the Glasgow Cup. However, in the league, they were much indebted to the goalscoring of Sandy McMahon. In the heart of the defence stood the magnificent James Kelly at centre-half, Joe Cullen was in goal and the charismatic Dan Doyle played at left-back. Willie Maley, although plagued by injury during the campaign, also played his part in the success.

Scottish League 1892–93

		Home					Away					
	P	W	D	L	F	A	W	D	L	F	A	Pts
1. Celtic	18	8	0	1	32	14	6	1	2	22	11	29
2. Rangers	18	7	2	0	22	13	5	2	2	19	14	28
3. St Mirren	18	6	1	2	29	14	3	1	5	11	25	20
4. Third Lanark	18	5	0	4	31	20	4	1	4	22	19	19
5. Heart of Midlothian	18	4	2	3	21	15	4	0	5	18	27	18
6. Leith Athletic	18	5	1	3	23	11	3	0	6	13	20	17
7. Dumbarton	18	5	1	3	21	12	3	0	6	14	23	17
8. Renton	18	4	2	3	17	17	1	3	5	14	27	15
9. Abercorn	18	5	0	4	24	17	0	1	8	11	35	11
10. Clyde	18	1	1	7	14	22	1	1	7	11	33	6

Renton re-elected, St Bernard's and Dundee elected in place of Abercorn and Clyde

🏴 BOYD SCORES FOR BRAZIL 🏴

When Scotland played Brazil in the 1998 World Cup finals, Tom Boyd scored an own goal to give Brazil a 2–1 win. John Collins, then at AS Monaco, scored a penalty for Scotland on 38 minutes after Cesar Sampaio scored the opener for Brazil just four minutes into the game.

🏴 CHOCCY'S CUP DOUBLE 🏴

In 1985, Brian McClair won the Scottish FA Cup with Celtic. Nine years later, he scored the fourth goal of the game in a 4–0 win over Chelsea at Wembley to give Manchester United their first-ever Double.

❦ THE CORONATION CUP SONG ❦

Said Lizzie to Philip as they sat down to dine
I've just had a note from a good friend of mine
His name is big Geordie, he's loyal and true
And his big dirty nose is a bright shade of blue
He says that the Rangers are right on their game
And he asks for a trophy to add to their fame
We'll send them a trophy that the Rangers can win
Said Philip to Lizzie, "Watch the Celts don't step in"
Said Lizzie to Philip, "They don't stand a chance
I'll send up my Gunners to lead them a dance
With the Celtic defeated, the way will be clear
And a trophy for the Rangers in my crowning year"
Alas, and alas, for the wearers of blue
The Celts beat the Arsenal and the Manchester too
Beat Hibs in the final, and lo and behold
All of Hampden was covered in green, white and gold
Said Lizzie to Philip when she heard the news
"So tell me dear Philip, for you ought to know
How to beat Glasgow Celtic and keep them below"
Said Philip to Lizzie, "There's only one way
And I've known the secret for many a day
To beat Glasgow Celtic, you'll have to deport
All the fighting mad Irish that give them support"

❦ FIVE CELTS SIGN FOR RANGERS ❦

On 11 March 1959, a Celtic/Rangers Select XI side played at Telford
Park, Inverness, to commemorate the switching on of Caledonian
FC's new floodlight system. However, at the time, SFA regulations
required all competing players to be signed to a single Scottish League
member club, so the five Celts that had been selected to play signed
for Rangers and then re-signed for Celtic the following day. The team
played in a kit of white shirts with blue and red hoops and white
shorts. The Celtic players to feature that day were Andrew Beattie,
Jim Kennedy, Charlie Tully, Paddy Crerand and Jim Conway.

❦ TURKU GOBBLED UP ❦

In the first round of the 1973–74 European Cup, Celtic met the
Finnish side, TPS Turku. Celtic easily disposed of the Scandinavians,
winning 9–1 on aggregate (3–0 and 6–1).

❧ CELTIC XI OF THE 1890s ❧

Reserves
Joe *CULLEN* • Jeremiah *REYNOLDS* • Peter *DOWDS*
Mick *DUNBAR* • David *STORRIER*
Manager
Willie *MALEY*

Did You Know That?
Celtic achieved their record victory, 11–0, against Dundee in 1895.

❧ THE BHOYS ARE BACK IN TOWN (1) ❧

"We knew, within ourselves, our own ability and we started to believe in ourselves but we never, ever, thought for one minute that we would win the European Cup."
***Jimmy Johnstone**, in 1995, on the players' assessment of their chances of winning the European Cup at the start of the 1966–67 season.*

❧ SUTTON'S ONE AND ONLY ❧

Chris Sutton came on as a substitute for Paul Scholes when he won his first, and only, England cap, against Cameroon at Wembley on 15 November 1997. He played for only ten minutes, was not selected for the England 1998 World Cup finals squad and later refused to play a "B" international; it ultimately spelt the end of his England career.

⚜ MADRID MADNESS ⚜

In the first leg of the 1974 European Cup semi-final, Celtic drew 0–0 with Atletico Madrid at Celtic Park. Celtic knew they were in for a bruising encounter when, a few days before they left Madrid for Glasgow, photos of two of Atletico's Argentinian players fighting during a training session were seen all over the sports pages in Madrid. Despite having lumps kicked out of them for the full 90 minutes, Celtic were the only team that night attempting to play any football. Only seven minutes had elapsed before the first Atletico played was booked – following a vicious assault on Jimmy Johnstone. After having brandished the yellow card ten times, Mr Babacan sent off the first Atletico player midway through the second half. By the end of the game, Madrid had been reduced to eight players, five of whom, including their goalkeeper, had been booked.

Despite a public outcry for Celtic not to play the second leg, the Celtic board decided to travel to Madrid rather than to risk retribution from UEFA should they have failed to fulfil the fixture. Celtic trained at Atletico's Vicente Calderon Stadium under the watchful eyes of several heavily armed policemen, with Jimmy Johnstone, who had received a death threat, watched even more closely. Celtic lost 2–0 in Madrid in front of 64,000 passionate home supporters and Atletico went through to the final in Brussels.

An article in *World Soccer* magazine summed up the two legs: "What a shame it is that a team from Madrid have to leave the fans with such cruel feelings and agonizing memories. Up until the Parkhead first-leg fiasco, Madrid had always thrown up visions of the legendary Real, with di Stefano gliding through the centre, Gento sweeping magnificently down the wing, Puskas and his lethal shooting power, the towering defensive work of Santamaria. One giant, ugly, clumsy foot has trodden these cherished memories well and truly into the dirt."

⚜ INTER JOY AND SADNESS ⚜

Celtic beat Inter Milan in the 1967 European Cup final and then went on to lose to them in the semi-final of the same competition in 1972.

⚜ CELTIC 4 JUVENTUS 3 ⚜

On 31 October 2001, Celtic beat Juventus 4–3 in a Champions League tie at Celtic Park.

✿❧ OUR BHOYS HAVE WON THE CUP (1) ❧✿

In 1892, Celtic won the Scottish Cup for the first time. The final, on 12 March, was against Queen's Park at Ibrox, but the game had to be declared a "friendly" because of persistent crowd encroachment. It was re-arranged for 9 April and turned out to be a very one-sided game, with Celtic's devastating pair of Johnny Campbell and Sandy McMahon scoring two goals each. Press reports comment on the massive support for Celtic in the crowd and the loud cheering at the end. For days afterwards, the Irish quarter of Glasgow was one huge party, with the cry of "Our Bhoys Have Won The Cup" echoing around the streets.

SCOTTISH FA CUP FINAL 1892
9 APRIL 1892, IBROX

Celtic (0) 5   v   **Queen's Park** (1) 1
(Campbell 2, McMahon 2,   (Waddell)
Sillars (o.g.))

Att. 20,000

Celtic: Cullen, Doyle, Reynolds, Gallagher, Kelly, W. Maley, Campbell, Dowds, McCallum, McMahon, Brady.

✿❧ FIRST SCOTTISH DOUBLE SUBSTITUTION ❧✿

On 11 December 1968, Celtic's Bobby Murdoch, making only his seventh appearance for his country, scored in Scotland's 5–0 away win over Cyprus in a World Cup qualifying group 7 game. He was the only Celtic player in the starting line-up, although he was later joined in the game by his club team-mates, Bobby Lennox and Billy McNeill, who came on as substitutes. It was the first time that Scotland had used two substitutes in an official international. .

✿❧ ITALIAN GIANTS BEAT CELTIC ❧✿

Celtic met AC Milan twice in the Champions League in the 2004–05 season. They lost 1–3 in the San Siro and drew 0–0 at Celtic Park.

✿❧ FIFTEEN TITLES ❧✿

In the same year that Celtic won their 15th Scottish League championship title, 1919, Glasgow-born Arthur Whitten Brown, along with John W. Alcock from England, became the first two aviators to cross the Atlantic Ocean; Alcock and Brown made the historic crossing eight days ahead of Charles Lindbergh.

❧ CELTIC'S NICKNAMES ❧

Celtic have several nicknames:
"The Bhoys" ❖ "The Hoops" ❖ "The Tims"

❧ CELTIC DENIED TRIPLE CUP TRIUMPH ❧

Hearts beat Celtic 4–3 at Ibrox Park in the 1901 Scottish FA Cup final to deny them a third consecutive victory in the competition.

❧ MACARI – EUROPE'S TOP GOALSCORER ❧

Celtic were knocked out of the 1971–72 European Cup by the eventual losing finalists, Inter Milan. There was some consolation, however, as Lou Macari topped the goalscoring charts in the competition, along with Taka from Standard Liege, with five goals.

❧ DANNY McGRAIN'S TESTIMONIAL ❧

In 1980, Celtic played Manchester United in a testimonial game for their long-serving captain, Danny McGrain. The game ended 0–0.

❧ GREEN AND BLUE MOJO ❧

Mo Johnston[†] was a prolific goalscorer for every club he played for:

Partick Thistle	41 goals	85 games	1981–83
Watford	23 goals	38 games	1983–84
Celtic	55 goals	99 games	1984–87
Nantes	22 goals	66 game	1987–90
Rangers	31 goals	76 games	1990–93
Everton	10 goals	34 games	1993–94
Hearts	5 goals	35 games	1994–95
Falkirk	1 goal	10 games	1985–96
Kansas City Wizards	30 goals	138 games	1996–2001
Scotland	13 goals	37 games	1984–92

❧ GOING UNDERGROUND ❧

In the same year that Celtic won their third Scottish League championship title, 1896, Glasgow's Underground was officially opened.

[†] Mo Johnston became Scotland's most expensive striker when Celtic paid Watford £400,000 for him.

❧ BERTIE AULD ❧

There is something quintessentially Celtic about Bertie Auld. A gallus Glaswegian boy, who had a tendency to self-destruct now and again but who also had, on occasion, an almost superhuman ability, Bertie was the Bhoy who the fans would identify with: the one who seemed to sum up everything about Celtic. How good it is that he is mentioned in the Willie Maley song "Murdoch, Tully, Johnstone, Auld and Hay"! He is certainly a Celt through and through.

Bertie's religious credentials would have suited Rangers, but once he arrived at Parkhead in 1955, there was no doubt that Celtic was his team. A talented left-winger, he might have played in the 7–1 Scottish Cup final win in 1957 – as he had played in the quarter-finals and the semi-final – but the nod was given to Neil Mochan. Bertie may have been disappointed, but his greatest moments for the club were still to come.

As a result of his poor disciplinary record and his general insubordination to the autocratic regime, Bertie repeatedly incurred the displeasure of the Celtic Board and, when Celtic reached the 1961 Scottish Cup final, his name was absent from the team sheet. Jock Stein, Dunfermline's manager at the time, was delighted and Celtic lost. Days later, Bertie was sold to Birmingham City for £15,000. During his time there, Bertie played in a Fairs Cup final and picked up a League Cup-winners' medal. In mid-January 1965, Bertie re-joined Celtic prior to the Big Man, Jock Stein's, dynasty. Indeed, it was Big Jock who had made the crucial decision to play Auld inside and to allow Bobby Lennox to run the left wing.

However, the greatest day in Bertie's career came in Lisbon and it was he who started the singing of "Sure, it's a grand old team" in the tunnel to terrify the slick, urbane Italians. Come the final whistle, the whole of Italy knew that it was indeed a grand old team. Celtic's America tour in the summer of 1970 was the catalyst for Bertie's departure from Celtic Park. He and Tommy Gemmell were sent home by acting manager Sean Fallon for indiscipline and, in 1971, he joined Hibs on a free transfer. In 1972, he came on as a substitute for Hibs in the Dixie Deans Cup final to a tremendous cheer from the Celtic fans who still loved him.

He later managed Partick Thistle (twice), Hibs and Dumbarton, but it is with Celtic that he will forever be associated.

Did You Know That?
During the 1965 Scottish Cup final against Dunfermline, Bertie Auld scored both equalizing goals for Celtic before Billy McNeill's winner. Seconds before the final whistle, to waste time, Bertie insisted that the police on duty remove their overcoats before he took a corner kick. The final whistle blew and Bertie raised both arms to exultant Celtic fans.

❧ MILLER THE THIRD ☙

When Celtic signed Kenny Miller from Wolverhampton Wanderers on 19 January 2006, he became only the third post war player to appear for both Old Firm clubs, following in the footsteps of Alfie Conn and Mo Johnston. In 2000, Miller left Hibernian in a £2 million deal for an unsuccessful spell with Rangers.

❧ FOUR STRAIGHT EURO QUARTER-FINALS ☙

Celtic reached the quarter-finals in one of the three major European competitions for four consecutive years, from 1969 to 1972.

Did You Know That?
Borussia Moenchengladbach's eight straight quarter-final appearances in one of the European competitions, from 1973 to 1980, is the record.

❧ HAPPY ANNIVERSARY ☙

Celtic celebrated their 50th anniversary in 1938 by winning the Scottish League championship and the Empire Exhibition Cup.

❧ MO JOHNSTON BRANDED "A JUDAS" ☙

In 1989, former Celtic hero, Maurice "Mo" Johnston, was playing for Nantes in the French league. Celtic were in negotiations to bring Mo back to Celtic Park, where he had scored 55 goals in 99 games wearing the Hoops' shirt between 1984 and 1987. At the time, Mo had said that if he returned to Scottish football it would be with Celtic, the team he supported as a boy. Following encouragement from the Celtic board, he even agreed to appear at a live press conference, announcing to the world that he was going back home to Celtic. However, enter Rangers and Graeme Souness, who made Mo a financial offer he could not refuse. So, in 1989, Mo Johnston signed for Rangers; it was a move that infuriated both sets of Old Firm fans. Rangers fans appeared on television and were seen burning their season tickets and scarves in bitter protest at the signing of not only a Roman Catholic but also a former Celtic player. On the other side of football's religious divide in Glasgow, Celtic fans felt betrayed by their "Prodigal Son", and labelled him the greatest football "Judas Iscariot" in history. Consequently, Mo Johnston became the first big-name Catholic star to play for Glasgow Rangers and the first Catholic signed by the club since the Second World War.

❧ CORONATION CUP WINNERS ❧

The Coronation Cup was a one-off football tournament to celebrate the coronation of Queen Elizabeth II in 1953 between four English clubs and four Scottish clubs – Aberdeen, Celtic, Hibernian and Rangers (Double winners in 1953) representing Scotland, and Arsenal, Manchester United, Newcastle United and Tottenham Hotspur representing England. All of the games were played at Ibrox Park and Hampden Park. On 11 May 1953, Celtic beat Arsenal 1–0, courtesy of a Bobby Collins goal direct from a corner kick in the 23rd minute of the game. Although Arsenal had just lifted the English First Division championship title, Celtic easily swept them aside and the scoreline would have been bigger had it not been for a Man of the Match performance from Arsenal's goalkeeper. On 16 May 1953, Celtic beat Manchester United 2–1 in front of 73,000 fans to progress to the final where they would be up against Hibernian, winners of the Scottish First Division in the previous two seasons. However, even Hibernian's "Famous Five" forward line of Smith, Johnstone, Reilly, Turnbull and Ormond were no match for Celtic, who, on 20 May 1953, ran out 2–0 winners in front of 117,060 fans at Hampden Park. Neilly Mochan scored after 28 minutes with a 35-yard thunderbolt and, with just three minutes remaining on the clock, Jimmy Walsh scored Celtic's second goal and the cup was won.

❧ CHALMERS CATCHES BRAZIL COLD ❧

On 25 June 1966, Celtic's Stevie Chalmers scored a goal in less than a minute for Scotland against Brazil in a friendly international in front of 74,933 fans at Hampden Park. The game ended 1–1 with Servilo scoring an equalizer for the two-time World Cup winners in the 15th minute. Chalmers' Celtic Park team-mate John Clark won his first Scotland cap in the game.

❧ CELTIC'S HALL OF FAME ❧

The following 25 players were inducted into the Glasgow Celtic Hall of Fame at the inaugural dinner in Glasgow on Saturday, 22 September 2001: Pat Bonner, Tom Boyd, Tommy Burns, Stevie Chalmers, John Clark, Bobby Collins, Dixie Deans, Sean Falon, Patsy Gallacher, David Hay, Paul Lambert, Jimmy Johnstone, Joe McBride, Danny McGrain, Jimmy McGrory, Murdo MacLeod, Billy McNeill, Billy McPhail, Paul McStay, Neil Mochan, Lubo Moravcik, Ronnie Simpson, Johnny Thomson, Charlie Tully, Willie Wallace.

❧ RUNNERS-UP STALEMATE ❧

In August 2003, Celtic, the Scottish Premier League runners-up, met Arsenal, the English Premier League runners-up, in a friendly at Celtic Park. The game ended 1–1.

❧ BIRTH CERTIFICATE MIX-UP ❧

Former Celtic striker, Tony Cascarino, represented the Republic of Ireland at international level 88 times and scored 19 goals. He was in Big Jack's side at the 1988 European Championships and the 1990 and 1994 World Cup Finals. Tony qualified to play for the Irish through his Irish grandmother. Amazingly after his 66th game for the Republic, it was discovered that Tony's grandmother had actually been adopted and only was brought up in Ireland and, therefore, Tony did not actually qualify to play for the Irish. Tony planned to be a hairdresser before he became a footballer and went on to play for Gillingham, Millwall, Aston Villa, Chelsea, Olympique Marseilles and Nancy as well as Celtic. After he retired from playing he commentated for TalkSPORT and wrote a column for *The Times*

❧ A CLEAN SWEEP ❧

Glasgow Celtic Football Club entered the *Guinness Book of Records* on 25 May 1967 by beating Inter Milan 2–1 in the 1967 European Cup final in Lisbon. In lifting the Cup, Celtic became:

* The first British team to win the European Cup
* The first "non-Latin" team to win the European Cup
* The first team to win the European Cup with homegrown players
* The first team to complete a "clean sweep" of every competition they entered in one year:[†] the Scottish First Division, Scottish FA Cup, Glasgow Charity Cup, Scottish League Cup and they even won the 1967 BBC Quiz Ball.

❧ SEVEN BEFORE CELTIC IN THE FA CUP ❧

Seven teams won the Scottish FA Cup before Celtic first picked up the trophy in 1892: Queen's Park, Vale of Leven, Dumbarton, Renton, Hibernian, Third Lanark and Hearts.

[†] *Jock Stein joked at the time that Celtic would have won the Derby at Epsom Downs too, but that the authorities wouldn't let Bobby Lennox run in it. This was the Big Man's testimony to Bobby's lightning speed, a gift that saw him wrongly flagged for offside on many occasions.*

✿ WE ARE THE CHAMPIONS (2) ✿

The 1904–05 season was the first and only time that a play-off was held to decide the Scottish League championship. The game, between Celtic and Rangers – who had a superior goal difference to their Glasgow rivals – was held at Hampden Park. Celtic had already beaten Rangers in the Glasgow Cup final, but had lost to them in the Scottish Cup semi-final. However, Quinn set up both goals, for McMenemy and Hamilton, as the Celtic faithful "danced on the cinders", singing "songs of their childhood". It would, of course, be the first of six consecutive league championships.

Scottish League 1904–05
First Division

| | P | Home | | | | | Away | | | | | Pts |
		W	D	L	F	A	W	D	L	F	A	
1. Celtic	26	8	4	1	31	15	10	1	2	37	16	41
2. Rangers	26	10	1	2	49	17	9	2	2	34	11	41
3. Third Lanark	26	11	1	1	48	12	3	6	4	12	16	35
4. Airdrieonians	26	6	4	3	23	18	5	1	7	15	27	27
5. Hibernian	26	7	5	1	27	11	2	3	8	12	28	26
6. Partick Thistle	26	8	0	5	20	20	4	2	7	16	36	26
7. Dundee	26	8	2	3	26	8	2	3	8	12	24	25
8. Heart of Midlothian	26	10	0	3	30	13	1	3	9	13	31	25
9. Kilmarnock	26	8	2	3	16	17	1	3	9	13	28	23
10. St Mirren	26	4	4	5	17	15	5	0	8	16	21	22
11. Port Glasgow Ath	26	6	3	4	23	20	2	2	9	7	28	21
12. Queen's Park	26	5	3	5	18	19	1	5	7	10	26	20
13. Morton	26	6	3	4	16	12	1	1	11	11	36	18
14. Motherwell	26	4	1	8	13	26	2	1	10	15	27	14

Championship Play-off
6 May 1905, Hampden Park
CELTIC 2 RANGERS 1

Falkirk and Aberdeen elected to the First Division, division increased to 18 clubs.

✿ CELTIC 8 PARTICK THISTLE 1 ✿

In the 1969–70 season, Celtic beat Partick Thistle 8–1 in the Scottish First Division to record their biggest-ever win over the Glasgow side.

🐝 THE BHOYS ARE BACK IN TOWN (2) 🐝

"He's all right financially, but I know millionaires who want to add more and more. He could have gone to other clubs that couldn't give him trophies. That's him."
Gordon Strachan, after signing Roy Keane

🐝 EMPIRE EXHIBITION TOURNAMENT 🐝

The Empire Exhibition tournament was played in the pre-war summer of 1938 to mark the Empire Exhibition being held in Bellahouston Park, Glasgow. Eight teams – four from Scotland (Aberdeen, champions Celtic, Hearts and Rangers) and four from England (Brentford, Chelsea, Everton and champions Sunderland) – participated in the tournament, which took place at Ibrox Park. Celtic played Sunderland in the first round and won a replay 3–1, after their first encounter ended in a 0–0 draw. In the semi-final, Celtic beat Hearts thanks to a Johnny Crum goal. Everton, who went on to win the English league championship in 1938–39, were Celtic's opponents in the final; Everton had already beaten Rangers 2–0 and Aberdeen 3–2 to reach the final and were the hot favourites to lift the cup. However, Johnny Crum scored the vital goal once again, five minutes into extra time, to win the game and the Empire Exhibition Cup for Celtic in front of 80,000 ecstatic supporters. The trophy, retained permanently by the winning club, was a silver replica of the Exhibition Tower.

🐝 EUROPEAN PENALTY SHOOT-OUT 🐝

Celtic have played in two European ties that have been settled by a penalty shoot-out and have lost on both occasions:

European Cup, semi-final, 1971–72
Internazionale (ITA) v. Celtic, 0–0 and 0–0 (lost 5–4 on penalties)
UEFA Cup, third round, 2001-02
Valencia (ESP) v. Celtic, 1–0 and 0–1 (lost 5–4 on penalties)

🐝 CLUB INFORMATION 🐝

Founded: 1888
Ground: Celtic Park (*also known as "Paradise"*)
Capacity: 60,832
Club colours: Emerald green-and-white hooped jerseys, white shorts with emerald green trims, and white socks

🦀 CELTIC XI OF THE 1900s 🦀

Reserves
Tom *SINCLAIR* • Willie *ORR* • David *MCLEAN*
Willie *KIVLICHAN* • Bobby *TEMPLETON*
Manager
Willie *MALEY*

Did You Know That?
This line-up was the actual all-conquering 1908 side. Celtic
currently hold the UK record for an unbeaten run in professional
football, 62 games (49 wins, 13 draws), between 13 November 1915
and 21 April 1917, or 17 months and 4 days.

🦀 FOUR BHOYS BEAT WORLD CHAMPS 🦀

On 15 April 1967, Scotland visited Wembley Stadium to play
England in a Home International and European Championship
group 8 game. England had not been beaten since their victory in
the World Cup final against West Germany that had taken place
in the same stadium nine months earlier. Four Celtic players were
in the Scotland team that beat the world champions 3–2 that day,
including goalkeeper Ronnie Simpson in goal, who was making his
international debut. Bobby Lennox scored along with Denis Law and
Jim McCalliog, who, like Simpson, was making his international
debut. Jackie Charlton and Geoff Hurst scored England's goals.

❧ ROLL OF HONOUR ☙

European Cup
Champions:..1966–67
Finalists:..1969–70
Semi-finals: 1971–72, 1973–74
Quarter-finals:...........1968–69, 1970–71, 1979–80

UEFA Cup
Finalists:...2002–03
Quarter-finals:...2003–04

Scottish League champions (40 times)
1892–93, 1893–94, 1895–96, 1897–98, 1904–05, 1905–06,
1906–07, 1907–08, 1908–09, 1909–10, 1913–14, 1914–15,
1915–16, 1916–17, 1918–19, 1921–22, 1925–26, 1935–36,
1937–38, 1953–54, 1965–66, 1966–67, 1967–68, 1968–69,
1969–70, 1970–71, 1971–72, 1972–73, 1973–74, 1976–77,
1978–79, 1980–81, 1981–82, 1985–86, 1987–88, 1997–98,
2000–01, 2001–02, 2003–04, 2005–06

Scottish FA Cup (33 times)
1891–92, 1898–99, 1899–00, 1903–04, 1906–07, 1907–08,
1910–11, 1911–12, 1913–14, 1922–23, 1924–25, 1926–27,
1930–31, 1932–33, 1936–37, 1950–51, 1953–54, 1964–65,
1966–67, 1968–69, 1970–71, 1971–72, 1973–74, 1974–75,
1976–77, 1979–80, 1984–85, 1987–88, 1988–89, 1994–95,
2000–01, 2003–04, 2004–05

Scottish League Cup (13 times)
1956–57, 1957–58, 1965–66, 1966–67, 1967–68, 1968–69,
1969–70, 1974–75, 1982–83, 1997–98, 1999–00, 2000–01,
2005–06

❧ CELTIC WIN OLD FIRM CUP FINAL REPLAY ☙

In the 1971 Scottish Cup final[†], Celtic beat Rangers 2–1 in a replay.
Derek Johnstone became the first substitute to score in the Scottish
Cup final, scoring Rangers' only goal of the replay.

[†]*Although the Scottish FA Cup was first competed for in 1874, substitutes were not permitted in
the final until 1968.*

🎵 OUR BHOYS HAVE WON THE CUP (2) 🎵

The 1904 Scottish Cup final is arguably Celtic's most famous Scottish Cup victory of them all and it was dominated by one man. Celtic were two down, but went in level at half-time thanks to two goals from Jimmy Quinn. Quinn scored again, to record the first hat-trick in a Scottish Cup final. It was the first big game at the new Hampden Park stadium, but Quinn was unfazed by the occasion, as he strolled up the pitch after scoring the third and winning goal. "Look at him! Cool as hell!" reported the *Glasgow Observer*. Dixie Deans equalled Quinn's hat-trick feat in the 1972 final.

SCOTTISH FA CUP FINAL 1904
16 APRIL 1904, HAMPDEN
Celtic (2) 3   v   **Rangers** (2) 2
(Quinn 3)   (Speedie 2)
Att. 64,323
Celtic: Adams, McLeod, Orr, Young, Loney, Hay, Muir, McMenemy, Quinn, Somers, Hamilton.

🎵 AWAY GOAL EUROPEAN EXITS 🎵

Celtic have lost four European ties on the away goals rule:

European Cup, third qualifying round, 2002–03
Celtic v. FC Basle (SUI), 3–1 and 0–2
(lost on the away goals rule)
UEFA Cup, first round, 1997–98
Celtic v. Liverpool (ENG), 2–2 and 0–0
(lost on the away goals rule)
European Cup-Winners' Cup, first round, 1989–90
Partizan Belgrade (YUG) v. Celtic, 2–1 and 4–5
(lost on the away goals rule)
European Cup-Winners' Cup, first round, 1980–81
Celtic v. Politehnica Timisoara (ROM), 2–1 and 0–1
(lost on the away goals rule)

🎵 CELTIC 19 RANGERS 18 🎵

Up to and including the 2005 final, Celtic have been runners-up in the Scottish FA Cup on 19 occasions to Rangers' total of 18. In 2005–06, neither Celtic nor Rangers reached even the quarter-finals, being knocked out by Clyde and Hibernian respectively.

❧ CELTIC LOSE TO HEAVY OUTSIDERS ☙

When Celtic met Aberdeen in the 1970 Scottish Cup final, they were very short-priced favourites to retain their trophy, having disposed of Rangers 4–0 in the previous year's final. However, Aberdeen upset all the odds by claiming a memorable 3–1 victory.

❧ CELTIC 8 STIRLING ALBION 0 ☙

On 6 November 2001, Celtic beat Stirling Albion 8–0 in the Scottish League Cup. The victory set a new record for Celtic's biggest win over Stirling Albion, having previously beaten them 7–3 in the 1958–59 season.

❧ CELTIC 7 HIBERNIAN 3 ☙

In the 1919–20 season, Celtic beat Hibernian 7–3 in the Scottish First Division to record their biggest-ever victory over the Edinburgh side.

❧ BROTHER WALFRID ☙

Glasgow Celtic were founded at a meeting held in St Mary's church hall, East Rose Street (now Forbes Street), Calton, Glasgow, on 6 November 1887 by Marist Brother Walfrid (real name Andrew Kerins), but they did not play their first game until 28 May 1888.[†] The purpose stated in the official club records for the formation of Glasgow Celtic Football Club was "to alleviate poverty in Glasgow's East End parishes". The charity established by Brother Walfrid was named "The Poor Children's Dinner Table". It was Brother Walfrid's idea to name the club "Celtic", as it was intended to reflect the club's Irish and Scottish roots.

❧ FIRST SCOTTISH CUP FINAL WIN ☙

Celtic won the Scottish Cup for the first time in 1892, following a 5–2 replay victory over Queen's Park. This was Celtic's second appearance in the final, having lost 2–1 in 1889 to Third Lanark in a replay. They were a notable scalp for Celtic, as Queen's Park were appearing in their tenth Scottish Cup final and had won their previous nine. The following year, Queen's Park collected the trophy for the tenth and last time in their history, beating Celtic 2–1 in the final.

[†] Unlike most clubs, Celtic built their ground first and then recruited a team to play in it.

❧ JOHN "DIXIE" DEANS ☙

John Deans was given the nickname "Dixie" in a conscious imitation of his near-namesake William Ralph Dean, who played for Everton and England between the wars. From the moment he arrived at Parkhead, he developed an instant affinity with the fans, despite the fact that he had been a Rangers supporter since his childhood.

In the autumn of 1971 his career was going nowhere fast. He had been with Motherwell for five years, but had been plagued by injury and had a bad disciplinary record. In his first ever visit to Parkhead as a Motherwell player, in December 1966, ironically on the same day that Willie Wallace made his Celtic debut, Deans was sent off. When Big Jock signed him in October 1971 for £17,500, he was actually serving a suspension. Stein was rebuilding Celtic, and Willie Wallace and John Hughes had recently departed to Crystal Palace, and so Stein looked to the chunky, but competitive, Deans to fill their place.

Dixie played his first game for Celtic on 27 November 1971, scoring a late goal in a 5–1 thrashing of Partick Thistle at Firhill. From then on, he was a regular goalscorer that season – teaming up perfectly with the talented, but as yet inexperienced, Kenny Dalglish. However, Dixie's relationship with the fans was put to the ultimate test when he was the only player out of ten who missed a penalty in the European Cup semi-final penalty shoot-out against Inter Milan on 19 April 1972. A section of the fans booed him off the pitch, but Dixie had the character to bounce back. Two weeks later, Dixie was a Celtic hero when he scored a hat-trick in the Scottish Cup final against Hibs, a feat that only the legendary Jimmy Quinn had previously achieved.

Dixie scored 27 goals for Celtic in the 1971–72 season at an average of more than one per game and, the following season, he found the net 32 times. That season, 1972–73, was the narrowest title win of the famous "nine-in-a-row". Many of Dixie's goals were simply "poachers' tap-ins", but he could head a goal, had a devastating shot and, surprisingly for a man of his build, an unexpected turn of speed. He scored twice in the game at Easter Road, including the goal that induced the delirium of the eighth successive league championship that turned Edinburgh green and white. The following season, he almost equalled Jimmy McGrory's feat of eight goals in a game when, on 17 November 1973, in a fixture against Partick Thistle, the cries of "Dixie! Dixie!" resounded around Parkhead. Dixie scored six times that day as McGrory watched from the stand. In the summer of 1976, Deans was off to Luton Town and then to Partick Thistle, Carlisle United and a brief spell in Australia.

❧ THE BHOYS ARE BACK IN TOWN (3) ❧

"We won and we won on merit. This win gives us more satisfaction than anything. I can still hardly believe it's true."
Jock Stein on Celtic's famous victory over Inter Milan

❧ CELTIC OWE HIBS A BIG THANK YOU ❧

Hibernian Football Club was founded by Irish immigrants in Edinburgh and, after Hibs had played benefit matches in Glasgow, the Irish community in Glasgow were inspired to found Glasgow Celtic along the same ideological lines. In 1886, Hibs were one of the best teams in Scotland and the founders of Celtic offered inducements to many of Hibs' best players to leave the Edinburgh club and to come to Glasgow to play for Celtic. These inducements included the tenancies of lucrative Glasgow public houses and were quite clearly in direct contravention of the amateur code that prevailed at the time. After several Hibs players had been persuaded to join Celtic, the Edinburgh club quickly declined and went out of business by the end of the season. They were re-founded the following year.

❧ SCOTLAND v. ENGLAND ❧

Celtic have met an English team on at least one occasion in all three major European competitions[†]:

> **European Cup**
> Leeds United .... (1969–70)
> **European Cup-Winners' Cup**
> Liverpool .... (1965–66)
> **UEFA Cup**
> Nottingham Forest .... (1983–84)
> Liverpool .... (1997–98 and 2002–03)
> Blackburn Rovers .... (2002–03)

❧ FOUR OFF IN OLD FIRM CLASH ❧

Four players were sent off when Rangers played Celtic in the 1991 Scottish Cup: Terry Hurlock, Mark Walters and Mark Hateley of Rangers and Peter Grant of Celtic.

[†] *Celtic have never met a team from Northern Ireland in any of the three major European competitions.*

❧ OUR BHOYS HAVE WON THE CUP (3) ☙

The 1913–14 season saw the emergence of another great Celtic team under the magical leadership of Willie Maley. The Double was secured, but it was the way that the Scottish Cup was won that marked the team out as something special. After a feckless first game, Celtic played Hibs off the park in the replay at Ibrox as Jimmy "Sniper" McColl and Johnny Browning each scored two goals. It is arguably one of Celtic's best-ever Scottish Cup final displays.

SCOTTISH FA CUP FINAL 1914
Replay (after 0–0 draw)
16 APRIL 1914, HAMPDEN PARK, GLASGOW
Celtic (3) 4   v   **Hibernian** (0) 1
(McColl 2, Browning 2)   (Smith)
Att. 36,000
Celtic: Shaw, McNair, Dodds, Young, Johnstone, McMaster;
McAtee, Gallacher, McColl, McMenemy, Browning.

❧ CELTIC 7 DUNDEE UNITED 0 ☙

In the 1919–20 season, Celtic beat Dundee United 7–0 to record their biggest-ever win over them.

❧ CAMBUSLANG ☙

Celtic have only played Cambuslang a total of four times in the Scottish First Division. In the 1891–92 season, Celtic won 3–1 at home and 4–0 away; in the 1892–93 season Celtic won 5–2 at home and lost 1–3 away.

❧ SCOTLAND v. WALES ☙

Celtic have met a Welsh team in one of the three major European competitions on just two occasions:

UEFA Cup
Inter Cardiff..(1997–98)
Cwmbran Town.......................................(1999–2000)

❧ CELTIC'S FIRST-EVER GAME ☙

On 28 May 1888, Celtic played their first game, beating Rangers 5–2.

❀❧ MAKE MINE A DOUBLE ❧❀

Celtic have won the domestic Double of Scottish League championship and Scottish FA Cup on 13 occasions:

1907, 1908, 1914, 1954, 1967, 1969, 1971,
1972, 1974, 1977, 1988, 2001, 2004.

❀❧ THE GLASGOW CUP ❧❀

For 100 years, between 1888 and 1988, senior SFA member clubs in the Glasgow area contested the Glasgow Football Association Cup. The Old Firm dominated the Glasgow Cup, winning the competition 73 times between them. After the Second World War, the Glasgow Cup lost a little of its shine as Scottish clubs concentrated less on it, focusing on the newly created European competitions being held instead. Following Rangers' win in 1971, the Glasgow Cup endured a three-year hiatus. It returned to the football calendar in the 1974–75 season, when it was shared for the first time in its history, as Celtic and Rangers drew 2–2 in the final. However, although taken lightly by the big clubs in its latter years, both teams put out their strongest sides whenever they reached the final. In 1986, on a Friday evening before the Scottish Cup final, a capacity crowd of just over 40,000 saw Rangers beat Celtic, the Scottish League champions, with a 3–2 win, thanks to an Ally McCoist hat-trick. In 1988, the Glasgow Cup was abandoned, before being resurrected as an Under-18 tournament.

❀❧ CELTIC MAKE THE NEWS ❧❀

In 1894, Celtic built the first-ever press box at Celtic Park. Other teams throughout the United Kingdom would later follow Celtic's pioneering example to bring football news to the community.

❀❧ HIBERNIAN DENY CELTIC IN CUP FINAL ❧❀

In 1902, Hibernian ended a miserable season for Celtic as the Edinburgh side ran out 1–0 winners in the Scottish FA Cup final played at Celtic Park. Rangers had already won their fifth league championship to pass Celtic's total for the highest number of championships won[†].

[†]Celtic missed out on achieving three consecutive Doubles in 1909 when the Scottish Football Association withdrew the award of the Scottish FA Cup following rioting by Celtic and Rangers fans at the Cup final that year.

🎽 THE DRYBOROUGH CUP 🎽

The Dryborough Cup was held from 1971 to 1980. It was played during the pre-season and was a straight knock-out tournament. The entrants were the eight teams that had scored the most Scottish First Division league goals during the previous season with the top four clubs seeded to avoid each other in the first round. When the Scottish Premier Division was established in 1974, the Drybrough Cup was put on hold. It was then reintroduced in 1979, with the four highest goal-scoring teams in the Scottish Premier Division plus the two highest-scoring teams in the Scottish First and Second Divisions invited. Celtic played a total of 16 games in the competition. Despite appearing in every Drybrough Cup final, with the exception of the last, Celtic only won the cup once. They beat Rangers 6–4 in a penalty shoot-out after the two sides had battled to a 2–2 draw in the 1974 final. Jimmy Johnstone scored the crucial penalty for Celtic.

🎽 FIRST CUP SUCCESS 🎽

Celtic won the Scottish FA Cup for the first time in the club's history in 1892. Up to 2006, Celtic have won it 33 times.

🎽 THIRD LANARK STEAL CELTIC'S THUNDER 🎽

In the 1903–04 season, Celtic and Rangers contested the Scottish FA Cup final at Hampden Park. The final had returned to its spiritual home after the four previous finals had been held at Celtic Park (two) and at Ibrox Park (two). Celtic won the final 3–2 to claim their fourth cup success, thereby equalling the four cups won by Rangers, although both clubs still trailed Queen's Park by six cup wins. However, it was Third Lanark who dominated the season, winning the Scottish championship for the first and only time in the club's history.

🎽 OLD FIRM PITCH BATTLE 🎽

On 10 May 1980, Celtic beat Rangers 1–0 after extra time in the Scottish Cup final at Hampden Park. Sadly, the game will be remembered more for fans fighting on the pitch than for the football that had been played. Following the game, the police called for all future matches between the Old Firm to be played behind closed doors, and their scheduled meeting in the Glasgow Cup final was postponed.

❧ THE TENNENTS SIXES ❧

Held from 1984 to 1993, the Tennents Sixes was an annual indoor football tournament contested in January each year by Scotland's senior clubs. The tournament was sponsored by Tennent Caledonian Breweries and was organized by the SFA. The inaugural tournament, in 1984, was contested at Coasters Arena in Falkirk, with Rangers claiming the cup. In 1985, the tournament moved to the Ingliston Showground near Edinburgh, and the remaining eight tournaments were all held at the Scottish Exhibition and Conference Centre in Glasgow. Along with Rangers, Aberdeen and Hearts both won the tournament twice, while Motherwell were the beaten finalists on four occasions. After Partick Thistle's success in 1993, Tennent Caledonian Breweries withdrew their sponsorship, thus bringing the curtain down on the event. Celtic's only win in the competition came in 1992.

❧ CLUB RECORDS ❧

Record victory.................................11–0, against Dundee in 1895
Record defeat.............................0–8, against Motherwell in 1937
Record points........72 *(Premier Division, 1987–88, two points for a win)*
　　　　　　　103 *(Premier League, 2001–02, three points for a win)*
Record home attendance.................92,000, against Rangers in 1938
Most Scotland caps...76, Paul McStay
Most appearances.................Billy McNeill, 486, from 1957–75
Most goals in a season.........................Jimmy McGrory, 50
Record scorer.......................................Jimmy McGrory, 550

❧ RECORD ATTENDANCE ❧

Celtic's Scottish Cup final win against Aberdeen FC in 1938 attracted a crowd of 146,433 – sometimes recorded as 147,365 – at Hampden Park. Either way, it is the highest ever attendance for a club football match in Europe.

❧ IBROX PARK CUP FINAL JOY ❧

In the 1911–12 season, Celtic won the Scottish FA Cup for the eighth time by beating Clyde 2–0 in the final at Ibrox Park. This was the second successive Scottish Cup final Celtic had won on their rival's territory, having disposed of Hamilton Academicals 2–1 in a replay in 1911.

❦ CELTIC PROTESTANT XI ❧

1
John
THOMSON

2
Danny
McGRAIN

4
Bobby
EVANS

5
Willie
LYON

3
Tommy
GEMMELL

6
Bertie
PEACOCK

7
Kenny
DALGLISH

8
Willie
WALLACE

10
Henrik
LARSSON

9
Dixie
DEANS

11
Bertie
AULD

Reserves
Davie *ADAMS* • Jimmy *YOUNG* • Jimmy *HAY*
Tom *McADAM* • Murdo *MacLEOD*
Manager
Jock *STEIN*

Did You Know That?

Over the past few years both Celtic and Rangers have attempted to combat Sectarianism amongst their fans. The Old Firm have worked hard to eradicate sectarianism.

❦ SCOTTISH FOOTBALL'S FIRST DOUBLE ❧

In the 1906–07 season, Celtic became the first Scottish club to win the Double[†] (Celtic beat Hearts 3–0 in the Scottish Cup final).

❦ RECORD-EQUALLING LEAGUE CUP WIN ❧

In the 1968–69 season, Celtic won their sixth Scottish League Cup to equal Rangers' record number of wins in the competition. Celtic beat Hibernian 6–2 at Hampden Park.

[†]*In 1907–08, Celtic won the Double for the second successive season (Celtic beat St Mirren 5–1 in the Scottish Cup final).*

❧ CELTIC MANAGERS ☙

Willie Maley ....(1897–1940)
Jimmy McStay ....(1940–45)
Jimmy McGrory ....(1945–65)
Jock Stein ....(1965–78)
Billy McNeill ....(1978–83)
David Hay..(1983–87)
Billy McNeill ....(1987–91)
Liam Brady ....(1991–93)
Lou Macari ....(1993–94)
Tommy Burns ....(1994–97)
Wim Jansen ....(1997–98)
Jozef Venglos ....(1998–99)
John Barnes ....(1999–2000)
Kenny Dalglish ....(2000)
Martin O'Neill ....(2000–05)
Gordon Strachan ....(2005–)

❧ MASS EXODUS OF TOP PLAYERS ☙

In the 1920–21 season, the Scottish League was hit by a mass
exodus of players leaving to join rival leagues. The SFA agreed to
allow Central and Western League teams to join a reformed Scottish
Second Division the following season.

❧ RECORD-EQUALLING CUP WIN ☙

Celtic won their tenth Scottish FA Cup in 1922–23 to equal Queen's
Park's record number of wins in the competition.

❧ A TALE OF THREE PARKS ☙

Celtic have won the Scottish FA Cup at two different Parks and lost
at three different Parks:

Celtic Park *(lost)* ❖ Hampden Park *(won and lost)*
Ibrox Park *(won and lost)*

❧ LAST OLD FIRM LEAGUE HAT-TRICK ☙

Stevie Chalmers was the last player to score a hat-trick in the league
in an Old Firm fixture when Celtic won 5–1 in January 1966.

🐝 WE ARE THE CHAMPIONS (3) 🐝

Celtic won the league championship in 1918–19 following their great players' return from the Great War – Jimmy McMenemy, Joe Dodds, Willie McStay, Joe Cassidy and Andy McAtee. They helped Celtic reclaim the title they had lost in 1918. Rangers pressed them hard, but Celtic's victories in their last two away fixtures, at Hearts and Ayr United, clinched the title. Andy McAtee scored in both games and was adored by the Celtic fans who sang:

The Kaiser, they say, only once saw him play
And remarked, it is said, "Dearie Me"
My German Artillery's just fit for the pillory
They can't shoot like young McAtee!

Scottish League 1918–19

| | | Home | | | | | Away | | | | | |
	P	W	D	L	F	A	W	D	L	F	A	Pts
1. Celtic	34	13	3	1	33	10	13	3	1	38	12	58
2. Rangers	34	15	2	0	51	7	11	3	3	35	9	57
3. Morton	34	10	7	0	49	20	8	4	5	27	20	47
4. Partick Thistle	34	11	1	5	38	21	6	6	5	24	22	41
5. Motherwell	34	7	5	5	28	19	7	5	5	23	21	38
6. Ayr United	34	9	1	7	34	22	6	7	4	28	31	38
7. Heart of Midlothian	34	8	5	4	31	20	6	4	7	28	32	37
8. Queen's Park	34	10	1	6	39	29	5	4	8	20	28	35
9. Kilmarnock	34	6	4	7	30	24	8	3	6	31	35	35
10. Clydebank	34	7	4	6	31	35	5	4	8	23	30	32
11. St Mirren	34	6	8	3	26	25	4	4	9	17	30	32
12. Third Lanark	34	4	4	9	27	34	7	5	5	33	28	31
13. Airdrieonians	34	4	7	6	21	26	5	4	8	24	28	29
14. Hamilton Academicals	34	6	2	9	23	31	5	3	9	26	44	27
15. Dumbarton	34	4	6	7	16	20	3	2	12	15	38	22
16. Falkirk	34	3	5	9	28	34	3	3	11	18	39	20
17. Clyde	34	4	4	9	23	33	3	2	12	22	42	20
18. Hibernian	34	5	0	12	16	35	0	3	14	14	56	13

Dundee, Raith Rovers and Aberdeen returned to active play, Albion Rovers elected to the league.

🐝 TEN IN 1910 🐝

In 1910, Celtic won their tenth Scottish League championship title.

❧ CELTIC, CELTIC ❧

Celtic, Celtic that's the team for me,
Celtic, Celtic on to victory,
They're the finest team in Scotland, I'm sure you will agree,
We'll never give up till we've won the cup and the Scottish
Football League
They come from bonnie Scotland, they come from county Cork,
They come from dear old Donegal and even from New York,
From every street in Glasgow, they proudly make their way,
To a place called dear old Paradise and this is what they say.

Celtic, Celtic that's the team for me,
Celtic, Celtic on to victory,
They're the finest team in Scotland, I'm sure you will agree,
We'll never give up till we've won the cup and the Scottish
Football League.

There's Fallon, Young and Gemmell who proudly wear the green,
There's Clark, McNeill and Kennedy the best there's ever been,
Jim Johnstone, Murdoch, Chalmers, John Divers and John Hughes,
And 60,000 Celtic fans who proudly shout the news.

Celtic, Celtic that's the team for me,
Celtic, Celtic on to victory,
They're the finest team in Scotland, I'm sure you will agree,
We'll never give up till we've won the cup and the Scottish
Football League.

❧ RECORD NUMBER OF CUP WINS ❧

Celtic won their 11th Scottish FA Cup in 1924–25 to move past the
record number of wins previously shared with Queen's Park (ten).

❧ CELTIC PARK HOSTS SCOTTISH CUP FINAL ❧

Celtic Park has played host to the Scottish FA Cup final five times:

1902	Hibernian 1–0 Celtic
1903	Rangers 2–0 Heart of Midlothian *(replay)*
1913	Falkirk 2–0 Raith Rovers
1993	Rangers 2–1 Aberdeen
1998	Hearts 2–1 Rangers

🎇 CELTIC MILESTONES 🎇

1887 .... The brainchild of Brother Walfrid, Celtic Football Club is formally constituted in St Mary's Church Hall in East Rose Street (now Forbes Street), Calton on 6 November 1887. The purpose is stated as being to alleviate poverty in Glasgow's East End parishes.

1888 .... Celtic beat Rangers 5–2 in a "friendly" on 28 May 1888. It is the club's first match and is played at the first Celtic Park.

1889 .... Celtic reach the Scottish Cup final in their first full season of competition, but lose 1–2 to the experienced Third Lanark. However, the season does not end in total disappointment, as Celtic collect their first trophy, the North-Eastern Cup (a local competition), beating Cowlairs 6–1 in the final.

1892 .... Celtic win the Scottish Cup for the first time in their history by defeating Queen's Park 5–2 in the final at Ibrox Park. A few months later, the club moves to its present ground.

1893 .... Celtic win their first Scottish League championship.

1897 .... The club becomes a private limited liability company, while Willie Maley is appointed secretary-manager.

1905–10 .... Celtic win the Scottish League championship for six successive seasons.

1907 .... Celtic achieve the first-ever domestic Double in Scotland by winning the Scottish Cup and the Scottish League championship in the same season.

1908 .... Celtic win their second successive Double.

1914–17 .... Celtic win the Scottish League championship four times in succession.

1937 .... Celtic beat Aberdeen in the Scottish Cup final, watched by a record crowd of 146,433 at Hampden Park.

1938 .... Celtic win the Empire Exhibition Trophy defeating Everton 1–0 in the final at Ibrox Park after extra time.

1940 .... Former player and ex-captain Jimmy McGrory replaces Jimmy McStay as manager.

1953 .... Celtic defeat Hibernian 2–0 in the Coronation Cup final. The competition was held to celebrate the coronation of Queen Elizabeth II and was contested by the top four teams in Scotland and England.

1956 .... Celtic win the Scottish League Cup for the first time in the club's history, defeating Partick Thistle 3–0 in a replay.

1957 .... Celtic retain the Scottish League Cup by hammering Rangers 7–1 in the final; it remains Celtic's best-ever win in an Old Firm game.

1964 .... In only their second season in European competition, Celtic reach the semi-final of the European Cup-Winners' Cup, going out 3–4 on aggregate to Hungary's MTK Budapest.

1965 .... Jock Stein succeeds Jimmy McGrory as manager of Celtic in March 1965 and guides the team to their first Scottish Cup success in 11 years.

1966 .... Celtic win the Scottish championship for the first time in 12 years and reach the semi-final of the European Cup-Winners' Cup again, before losing 1–2 on aggregate to Liverpool.

1967 .... Celtic complete their most glorious season in their history by winning every competition they enter: Scottish League, Scottish FA Cup, Scottish League Cup, Glasgow Cup and the ultimate club prize in European competition, the European Cup.

1970 .... Celtic reach the European Cup final again, but lose 2–1 to the Dutch champions Feyenoord after extra time in Milan. In the semi-final, Celtic beat Leeds United both home and away.

1972 .... Celtic reach the European Cup semi-final for the third time, but lose in heart-breaking fashion at Celtic Park to Inter Milan in a penalty shoot-out.

1974 .... Celtic win the Scottish League championship for the ninth season in a row; a joint world record at the time for success in a domestic league.

1977 .... Celtic win the Scottish League championship for the tenth and final time under Jock Stein's reign as manager. Celtic also achieve the Double, beating Rangers 1–0 in the Scottish Cup final at Hampden Park.

1978 .... Jock Stein steps down as Celtic manager and is succeeded by Billy McNeill, the captain of the 1967 European Cup-winning side. During Stein's 12 years in charge, excluding season 1975–76, when he was recuperating from injuries received in a car crash, Celtic won 25 trophies in major competitions: the European Cup (1), Scottish League championships (10), Scottish Cups (8) and Scottish League Cups (6).

1979 .... Billy McNeill guides Celtic to the Scottish championship in his first season as manager. Celtic win the title in dramatic fashion at Celtic Park with a 4–2 win over Rangers in the last match of the season.

1983 .... Billy McNeill is replaced as manager by David Hay.

1985 .... Celtic win the Scottish Cup by beating Dundee United 2–1 at Hampden Park in the 100th Scottish Cup final.

1986 .... Celtic snatch the Scottish championship by pipping Heart of Midlothian on the last day of the season. Celtic dramatically lifted the title on goal difference, beating St Mirren 5–0 at Love Street, while Hearts lost 0–2 to Dundee at Dens Park, with both Dundee goals coming in the final few minutes of the game.

1987 .... Billy McNeill returns to Celtic Park as manager, becoming the first man to have managed Celtic twice.

1988 .... Celtic celebrate their centenary season in 1987–88 by clinching the club's first Double in 11 years. It was Celtic's 35th championship success and their 28th Scottish Cup final win.

1989 .... Celtic win the Scottish Cup for the 29th time, beating Rangers in the final at Hampden Park.

1991 .... Liam Brady is appointed the new manager of Celtic replacing Billy McNeill. Brady becomes the first Celtic manager never to have played for the club.

1993 .... Liam Brady is replaced as Celtic manager by former player, Lou Macari.

1994 .... In March 1994, Fergus McCann takes control of a financially strained Celtic after ousting the board of directors. McCann replaces Lou Macari as manager with Tommy Burns. In late 1994, the club was reconstituted as a plc, a move that was quickly followed by the most successful share issue in the history of British football.

1995 .... Celtic play their home fixtures at Hampden Park during the 1994–95 season while Celtic Park undergoes reconstruction. The season they spend away from their spiritual home ends with a 1–0 win over Airdrieonians in the Scottish Cup final. It is Celtic's 30th Scottish FA Cup success and the club's first major trophy in six years.

1997 .... Wim Jansen replaces Tommy Burns as manager and guides Celtic to their first Scottish League Cup final victory for 15 years with a 3–0 win over Dundee United at Ibrox Park.

1998 .... Wim Jansen guides Celtic to Scottish championship success and prevents Rangers from bettering Celtic's run of nine successive titles. It is Celtic's first title win since 1988 but, shortly afterwards, Jansen leaves Celtic Park and is replaced by Dr Jozef Venglos.

1999 In April 1999, Fergus McCann leaves Celtic following the completion of his five-year plan. Allan MacDonald is appointed as Celtic's new chief executive. A few months later, Dr Venglos retires and is replaced by John Barnes. Kenny Dalglish, Celtic's new director of football operations, guides Barnes.

2000 John Barnes leaves the club in February 2000 following a humiliating 3–1 defeat at Celtic Park in the Scottish Cup by Inverness Caledonian Thistle. Kenny Dalglish takes control of first-team affairs until the end of the season. Celtic end the 1999–2000 season as championship runners-up to Rangers, 21 points adrift. However, Celtic do win the Scottish League Cup, thanks to a 2–0 victory over Aberdeen. Martin O'Neill is appointed as the new manager of Celtic during the summer. In his first Old Firm game, played at Celtic Park on 27 August 2000, Celtic hammer Rangers 6–2 in the league.

2001 In March 2001, Celtic collect their first piece of silverware under the reign of Martin O'Neill, retaining the Scottish League Cup after a 3–0 final victory over Kilmarnock, which includes a hat-trick from Henrik Larsson. In April 2001, Celtic are crowned Scottish League champions with five games to spare, having beaten Rangers at Ibrox Park in a league game for the first time in six years. By the end of the season, Celtic achieve the domestic Treble of Scottish League championship, Scottish League Cup and the Scottish Cup, following a 3–0 win over Hibernian in the final.

2003 Celtic finish the 2002–03 season without a trophy, losing to Inverness Caledonian Thistle in the Scottish Cup, to Rangers in the Scottish League Cup and lose the league championship by a goal-margin difference of just a single goal. In May, in Seville, Spain, Celtic lose 2–3 after extra time to Porto in the final of the UEFA Cup. It is Celtic's first European final in 33 years.

2005 Martin O'Neill steps down as manager in May and former Aberdeen player Gordon Strachan is appointed the new man in charge at Celtic Park. In December, former Manchester United legend Roy Keane signs for Celtic.

2006 In his first season in charge at Celtic Park, Gordon Strachan guides Celtic to Scottish CIS Cup and Scottish Premier League success.

🏵 WE ARE THE CHAMPIONS (4) 🏵

The 1925–26 season was a fantastic one for Celtic. The injury to, and virtual retirement of, Patsy Gallacher mattered little in the end as Willie Maley had brought Tommy McInally back to the club from Third Lanark. "We knew that he was pining for home," said Maley. His wizardry that season was something to behold, but the season also marked the emergence of a young centre-forward who had scored the winning goal in the 1925 Scottish Cup final. The player was, of course, Jimmy McGrory, who scored 32 league goals in 37 appearances that season as Celtic finished eight points clear of second-placed Airdrie.

Scottish League 1925–26
First Division

	P	HOME					AWAY					Pts
		W	D	L	F	A	W	D	L	F	A	
1. Celtic	38	15	4	0	59	15	10	4	5	38	25	58
2. Airdrieonians	38	13	3	2	53	22	10	1	8	42	32	50
3. Heart of Midlothian	38	14	2	3	52	21	7	6	6	35	35	50
4. St Mirren	38	12	4	3	37	23	8	3	8	25	29	47
5. Motherwell	38	15	1	3	41	15	4	7	8	26	31	46
6. Rangers	38	12	1	6	39	21	7	5	7	40	34	44
7. Cowdenbeath	38	14	3	2	54	20	4	3	12	33	48	42
8. Falkirk	38	8	10	1	35	21	6	4	9	26	36	42
9. Kilmarnock	38	11	4	4	49	30	6	3	10	30	47	41
10. Dundee	38	9	4	6	29	27	5	5	9	18	32	37
11. Aberdeen	38	10	4	5	35	23	3	6	10	14	31	36
12. Hamilton Academicals	38	10	5	4	40	29	3	4	12	28	50	35
13. Queen's Park	38	10	1	8	43	39	5	3	11	27	42	34
14. Partick Thistle	38	8	6	5	39	35	2	7	10	25	38	33
15. Morton	38	9	5	5	35	30	3	2	14	22	54	31
16. Hibernian	38	8	3	8	48	37	4	3	12	24	40	30
17. Dundee United	38	7	4	8	31	27	4	2	13	21	47	28
18. St Johnstone	38	5	8	6	22	31	4	2	13	21	47	28
19. Raith Rovers	38	9	2	8	30	30	2	2	15	16	51	26
20. Clydebank	38	7	3	9	37	33	0	5	14	18	59	22

Dunfermline Athletic and Clyde promoted.

🏵 JOCK'S CROWNING GLORY 🏵

Jock Stein captained Celtic's 1953 Coronation Cup winning team.

❧ THE BHOYS ARE BACK IN TOWN (4) ❧

"You could take all the derby matches in the world, and put them all together and they still wouldn't equal one-millionth of the Old Firm. There's nothing like it."
Paolo Di Canio, *2000*

❧ OLD FIRM CUP FINALS ❧

Since the first Scottish Cup final in 1874, the Old Firm has met in 15 finals with a record of seven victories each and one no contest. Here is a list of Old Firm Scottish FA Cup finals:

2002	Rangers 3–2 Celtic
1999	Rangers 1–0 Celtic
1989	Celtic 1–0 Rangers
1980	Celtic 1–0 Rangers *aet*
1977	Celtic 1–0 Rangers
1973	Rangers 3–2 Celtic
1971	Celtic 2–1 Rangers (replay)
1969	Celtic 4–0 Rangers
1966	Rangers 1–0 Celtic (replay)
1963	Rangers 3–0 Celtic (replay)
1928	Rangers 4–0 Celtic
1909	*Not awarded*[†]
1904	Celtic 3–2 Rangers
1899	Celtic 2–0 Rangers
1894	Rangers 3–1 Celtic

❧ FISH 'N' CHIPS ❧

In September 2005, Gordon Strachan and his wife were spotted in Montgomery Fish Bar, Edinburgh. Strachan had taken his wife Lesley along to see Hibernian play Dnipro Dnipropetrovsk (Ukraine) in the UEFA Cup and, after the game, they went for a fish supper at his favourite chippie in Edinburgh. Strachan, who was brought up on a council estate in Edinburgh, said the café was a favourite of his: "We had fish and chips outside Easter Road and a cup of tea. Lovely. Montgomery Café if you want nice fish and chips. It's brilliant." Although the café was packed with Hibs fans after the game, Gordon and his wife were left alone to enjoy their supper.

[†]The SFA withheld the cup after a riot at Hampden Park following the replay between Celtic and Rangers.

❧ JIMMY DELANEY ☙

Jimmy Delaney made 305 appearances for Celtic between 1934 and 1946 – many of them, sadly, in unofficial wartime competitions – and won two Scottish First Division championship-winners' medals, one Scottish Cup-winners' medal, one Empire Exhibition Trophy medal, one Glasgow Cup medal, three Glasgow Charity Cup medals and 13 Scottish caps.

Jimmy is unique in that he won a cup-winners' medal in Scotland, England and Northern Ireland, with Celtic in 1937, Manchester United in 1948 and Derry City in 1954. He almost achieved what would have been an even more unique quad, but his team, Cork Athletic, lost in the Football Association of Ireland (Republic of Ireland) Cup final to Shamrock Rovers in 1956. Jimmy also played for Aberdeen, Falkirk and Elgin City. During the Second World War, he served in Africa and Italy and, in April 1946, he scored a famous last-minute winner for Scotland against England in the Victory International.

Jimmy's great years for Celtic had been from 1934 to 1939, where Willie Maley deployed him on the right wing. Delaney was fast, direct, could cross and had the disconcerting ability to cut inside a defender and charge into the box. He could also take a goal, with perhaps his most famous goalscoring exploit being the hat-trick he scored against Rangers in the 1936 Glasgow Charity Cup final.

Celtic won the league in 1936 and 1938, and the forward line of Delaney, Buchan (or MacDonald), Crum, Divers and Murphy was one of the best in the history of the club. In 1937, a crowd of 146,433 watched Delaney inspire Celtic to victory over Aberdeen in the Scottish Cup; a week earlier, a packed house had seen Delaney inspire Scotland to victory over England. And then, in 1938, came the Empire Exhibition Trophy: "Fetch a polis [sic] man, Everton's getting murdered" was the cry in the final at Ibrox as Jimmy roasted Everton's defence.

In February 1946, Manchester United's new manager, Matt Busby, lured the 31-year-old to Old Trafford and, in 1948, he starred in United's FA Cup final triumph over Blackpool. However, during his time in Manchester, he would always look in the evening paper to see the Celtic result. In 1950, he returned to Scotland to play for Aberdeen and then moved on to Falkirk. Jimmy was always given a warm reception when he played for the opposition at Parkhead and, on one occasion, the Celtic crowd famously turned on their full-back Frank Meechan for fouling the great Jimmy. He then signed for Derry City before ending his career at Elgin City. He died in 1989.

❧ CELTIC AT HAMPDEN PARK UNVEILING ☙

At the beginning of the 1902–03 season, Queen's Park unveiled Hampden Park[†] as their home ground with their opening league match against Celtic. At the time, Hampden Park was regarded as the greatest stadium in the world.

❧ OLD FIRM RIOT AT CUP FINAL ☙

At the 1909 Scottish FA Cup final replay at Hampden Park, Old Firm fans ran riot at the end of the match. Both of the games had ended in a draw. On the pitch, as well as on the terraces, the players and fans assumed that extra time would be played to decide a winner. However, under the SFA rules at the time, extra time was only permissible at the end of a second replay. When the referee told the players to leave the pitch, the 60,000-strong crowd inside Hampden Park went crazy, believing that the two drawn games had been staged by the clubs to bring in additional revenue. Hundreds of fans ran onto the pitch and vented their anger by tearing down the goals, cutting up the turf and setting fire to the turnstiles and Main Stand, using whisky as fuel. Over 100 people were hurt during the rioting, many of them policemen and firemen. In the aftermath, the SFA took the decision to withhold the cup and the players' medals, while both clubs were ordered to pay the appropriate amount of compensation to Queen's Park Football Club, the owners of Hampden Park.

❧ PENALTY SHOOT-OUT MISERY ☙

Celtic are the only club in Scotland to have lost both a Scottish FA Cup final and a Scottish League Cup final in a penalty shoot-out. In 1990, Celtic drew 0–0 with Aberdeen at Hampden Park in the Scottish FA Cup final, going down 9–8 on penalties. In 1995, Celtic drew 2–2 with Raith Rovers at Ibrox Park in the Scottish League Cup final, going down 6–5 on penalties.

❧ SEVENTH HEAVEN ☙

In 1970, Celtic won their seventh Scottish League Cup final to set a new record for the greatest number of wins in the competition. Celtic beat St Johnstone 1–0 at Hampden Park.

[†]Hampden Park hosted the Scottish FA Cup final for the first time in 1904 with Celtic beating Rangers 3–2 in the final.

🎖 OUR BHOYS HAVE WON THE CUP (4) 🎖

In 1927, Celtic beat Second Division East Fife 3–1 in a very one-sided Scottish Cup final at Hampden Park. It was the first Scottish game to be broadcast on the radio. As the match neared its conclusion, Tommy McInally decided to mess about and show-off to his adoring fans, deliberately shooting high and wide. The press reported that McInally "delighted the now happy Celtic choristers with some shots of the balloon variety". Earlier in the week, a players' delegation had approached Willie Maley for a pay rise. Maley's curt reply was: "Get out and bring me back that cup."

SCOTTISH FA CUP FINAL 1927
16 APRIL 1927, HAMPDEN PARK, GLASGOW

Celtic (2) 3   v   **East Fife** (1) 1
(Robertson (o.g.), McLean,   (Wood)
Connolly)

Att. 80,070

Celtic: J. Thomson, W. McStay, Hilley, Wilson, J. McStay, McFarlane, Connolly, A.Thomson, McInally, McMenemy, McLean.

🎖 STREAKER REFEREE 🎖

Prior to Celtic's 2003 UEFA Cup final against Porto in Seville, Spain, on 21 May 2003, serial streaker Mark Roberts ran onto the pitch dressed in a fake referee's uniform which had been lightly secured with Velcro. When he approached the real referee, he flashed a red card in his face and took off his gear and then proceeded to dribble past the astonished Porto players with a football.

🎖 CELTIC 15 EAST FIFE 3 🎖

Celtic recorded their biggest-ever win over East Fife[†] in the 1930–31 season, beating them 9–1 at Celtic Park in a Scottish First Division match. In the same season, Celtic also beat East Fife 6–2 away.

🎖 KILLIE KILLED 🎖

Celtic inflicted Kilmarnock's heaviest-ever defeat when they beat them 9–1 on 13 August 1938 in a First Division game.

[†]*In 1938, East Fife became the first Second Division side to win the Scottish FA Cup, beating Kilmarnock 4–2 at Hampden Park in a replay.*

❧ CELTIC'S SCOTTISH CUP HISTORY ❧

Apart from their 15 Scottish Cup final appearances against Rangers, seven of which they won, Celtic have also appeared in 37 other Scottish Cup finals, winning 26 of them:

1889	Third Lanark 2-1 Celtic *replay*
1892	Celtic 5–1 Queen's Park *replay*
1893	Queen's Park 2–1 Celtic *replay*
1900	Celtic 4–3 Queen's Park
1901	Hearts 4–3 Celtic
1902	Hibernian 1–0 Celtic
1907	Celtic 3–0 Hearts
1908	Celtic 5–1 St Mirren
1911	Celtic 2–0 Hamilton Academicals *replay*
1912	Celtic 2–0 Clyde
1914	Celtic 4–1 Hibernian *replay*
1923	Celtic 1–0 Hibernian
1925	Celtic 2–1 Dundee
1926	St Mirren 2–0 Celtic
1927	Celtic 3–1 East Fife
1931	Celtic 4–2 Motherwell *replay*
1933	Celtic 1–0 Motherwell
1937	Celtic 2–1 Aberdeen
1951	Celtic 1–0 Motherwell
1954	Celtic 2–1 Aberdeen
1955	Clyde 1–0 Celtic *replay*
1956	Hearts 3–1 Celtic
1961	Dunfermline 2–0 Celtic *replay*
1965	Celtic 3–2 Dunfermline Athletic
1967	Celtic 2–1 Aberdeen
1970	Aberdeen 3–1 Celtic
1972	Celtic 6–1 Hibernian
1974	Celtic 3–0 Dundee United
1975	Celtic 3–1 Airdrieonians
1984	Aberdeen 2–1 Celtic *aet*
1985	Celtic 2–1 Dundee United
1988	Celtic 2–1 Dundee United
1990	Aberdeen 0–0 Celtic *aet, 9–8 penalties*
1995	Celtic 1–0 Airdrieonians
2001	Celtic 3–0 Hibernian
2004	Celtic 3–1 Dunfermline
2005	Celtic 1–0 Dundee United

⚽ AN INTER-WAR CELTIC XI ⚽

1
John
THOMSON

2
Alec
McNAIR

3
Jock
MORRISON

4
Peter
WILSON

5
Willie
LYON

6
George
PATERSON

7
Jimmy
DELANEY

8
Patsy
GALLACHER

9
Jimmy
McGRORY

10
Tommy
McINALLY

11
Adam
McLEAN

Reserves
Charlie *SHAW* • Willie *CRINGAN* • Joe *DODDS*
Frank *MURPHY* • Johnny *CRUM*
Manager
Willie *MALEY*

Did You Know That?
Celtic's 1938 Scottish Cup final win over Aberdeen at Hampden Park was attended by a crowd of 146,433, which remains a record for a European club match.

⚽ THE BHOYS ARE BACK IN TOWN (5) ⚽

"It is up to us, to everyone at Celtic Park, to build up our own legends. We don't want to live with history, to be compared with legends from the past. We must make new legends."
Jock Stein, after first winning the League with Celtic, May 1966.

⚽ BHOYS UNLUCKY 50TH ⚽

In 1906, Hearts won the Scottish FA Cup final for the fourth time in the club's history, with a 1–0 win over Third Lanark at Ibrox Park. Exactly 50 years later, Hearts beat Celtic 3–1 at Hampden Park to win their fifth Scottish Cup and their first in 50 years.

❧ SCOTTISH CUP – OLD FIRM FINALS ☙

Since the first Scottish Cup final in 1874, the Old Firm has met in 15 finals with a record of seven victories each and one no contest: Here is a list of Old Firm Scottish FA Cup finals:

1894..Rangers 3–1 Celtic
1899..Celtic 2–0 Rangers
1904..Celtic 3–2 Rangers
1909..*Not awarded*[†]
1928..Rangers 4–0 Celtic
1963..Rangers 3–0 Celtic *replay*
1966..Rangers 1–0 Celtic *replay*
1969..Celtic 4–0 Rangers
1971..Celtic 2–1 Rangers *replay*
1973..Rangers 3–2 Celtic
1977..Celtic 1–0 Rangers
1980..Celtic 1–0 Rangers *aet*
1989..Celtic 1–0 Rangers
1999..Rangers 1–0 Celtic
2002..Rangers 3–2 Celtic

[†]The SFA withheld the cup after a riot at Hampden Park following the replay. All of the games were played at Hampden Park.

❧ OLD FIRM LEAGUE ATTENDANCE RECORD ☙

In the 1938–39 season, the game between Rangers and Celtic at Ibrox Park attracted a crowd of 118,567 spectators, a record for a Scottish League match. Rangers won 2–1.

❧ OLD FIRM LOCKED OUT ☙

The 1951–52 season was a barren one for the Old Firm. Hibernian won their fourth league title, Dundee won their first League Cup (beating Rangers 3–2 in the final) and Motherwell lifted the Scottish FA Cup for the first time in the club's history (beating Dundee 4–0 in the final).

❧ 10 DOUBLE WINS ☙

Celtic achieved their tenth Double success in 1977 by beating Rangers 1–0 in the Scottish FA Cup final at Hampden Park. Celtic narrowly missed out on claiming their third Treble, as they lost the Scottish League Cup final to Aberdeen, going down 2–1 after extra time.

❧ TWO OUT OF THREE AIN'T BAD ❧

Celtic clinched the Treble in 1969, their second in just three years. A 6–2 hammering of Hibernian in the Scottish League Cup final was followed up by a sweet 4–0 Scottish Cup final win over Rangers.

❧ CELTIC 19 RANGERS 19 ❧

In Celtic's historic Treble-winning season of 1966–67, they drew level with Rangers in the table for the greatest number of Scottish FA Cup wins, winning their 19th cup by beating Aberdeen 2–1 in the final at Hampden Park[†].

❧ BIG JOCK FIGHTS THE CELTIC BOARD ❧

Prior to the start of the 1965–66 season, Jock Stein, who had been made the manager of Celtic in February 1965, took on Celtic's board of directors by insisting on having sole control when it came to selecting the team and stating that he would not accept a joint management role with Sean Fallon. Nothing like this had ever happened at Celtic Park before, but Big Jock got his way and Celtic not only won the Scottish League Cup in 1966, but were also crowned league champions. Celtic narrowly missed out on capturing their first-ever domestic Treble, losing the Scottish FA Cup final 0–1 to Rangers in a replay. However, Big Jock now made winning the European Cup his number one priority.

❧ DIOUF SPITS AT CELTIC FANS ❧

Eighty-seven minutes into Celtic's 1–1 draw with Liverpool in their 2003 UEFA Cup quarter-final, first-leg tie at Celtic Park, Liverpool's El Hadji Diouf tripped over an advertising hoarding in an attempt to keep the ball in play and tumbled into a section of the crowd. A number of Celtic fans helped him to his feet, with one fan patting him on the head, while many others laughed at the Senegalese international's misfortune. Then, after incessant booing, Diouf spat into the crowd. He was substituted three minutes later and walked straight down the tunnel. Strathclyde Police took statements from witnesses in the crowd and, after the game, UEFA handed Diouf a two-game ban and the Glasgow Sheriff Court fined him £5,000 for the incident.

[†]*In the 1968–69 season, Celtic moved into the outright lead for the highest number of Scottish FA Cup wins, claiming their 20th after their 4–0 win over Rangers in the final at Hampden Park.*

❧ JIMMY McSTAY ❧

In February 1940, Jimmy McStay left Alloa Athletic to take up the vacant manager's position at Celtic Park. McStay was an obvious candidate for the position, given that he was a former Celtic captain who had made over 450 appearances for the club. Jimmy also had strong family ties with Celtic Park: his brother Willie also played for Celtic and he was the great-uncle of future Celtic legend, Paul McStay. Unfortunately, Celtic did not enjoy much success under McStay and secured no major trophies to boast of during his five years in charge. However, it was thought that the appointment of Desmond White, son of the then-chairman Tom White, as club secretary prior to McStay's arrival, somewhat reduced both his position and his influence as manager. Ultimately, it was Celtic's board of directors that controlled the signing of players, and that can only have helped undermine McStay's position. The only players he could personally sign for the club were youth players. Looking back, it was those circumstances that were responsible for the barren years during McStay's time in charge. He became manager during the first wartime season and throughout his time as manager the city of Glasgow became increasingly involved in the war effort. Consequently, the importance of football soon slid down the list of priorities for most people in the city, including the Celtic board. In July 1945, McStay was forced to resign following a short meeting with the chairman; just as had been the case with his predecessor, Willie Maley. It is widely reported that McStay was one of the last people to hear about his dismissal, after which he told the *Sunday Mail*: "The whole affair has caused me much unjustified embarrassment."

Did You Know That?
After McStay vacated the manager's office at Celtic Park, it was not long before he was back at the club. He was a scout for his successor, Jimmy McGrory.

❧ CELTIC'S LONGEST-SERVING FOREIGNER ❧

Morten Wieghorst is Celtic's all-time longest-serving foreign player, excluding British and Irish players. He joined Celtic in December 1995 and left the club in 2002. Canadian goalkeeper Joe Kennaway spent almost a decade at Celtic Park back in the 1950s but, given that he was a native English speaker who was capped by Canada, Scotland and the USA, he cannot be included as a "foreigner".

✿✿ WE ARE THE CHAMPIONS (5) ✿✿

The Celtic team that lifted the Scottish League championship in 1935–36, after an interval of ten years, is generally considered to be one of the best in the club's history. It was the season in which Jimmy McGrory scored 50 league goals, but it was also the year that saw the emergence of a great right-winger, Jimmy Delaney, whose speed, crossing ability and directness were second to none – as was his gentlemanly demeanour both on and off the field. Celtic also had a great leader at centre-half, with Willie Lyon, while trainer Jimmy McMenemy also deserves much credit for having effectively run the team in Maley's old age.

Scottish League 1935–36
First Division

	P	HOME					AWAY					Pts
		W	D	L	F	A	W	D	L	F	A	
1. Celtic	38	17	1	1	71	16	15	1	3	44	17	66
2. Rangers	38	14	3	2	67	26	13	4	2	43	17	61
3. Aberdeen	38	15	3	1	52	19	11	6	2	44	31	61
4. Motherwell	38	12	3	4	46	25	6	9	4	31	33	48
5. Heart of Midlothian	38	14	4	1	56	20	6	3	10	32	35	47
6. Hamilton Academicals	38	11	4	4	56	31	4	3	12	21	43	37
7. St Johnstone	38	10	4	5	43	27	5	3	11	27	54	37
8. Kilmarnock	38	10	4	5	46	30	4	3	12	23	34	35
9. Third Lanark	38	11	4	4	47	29	4	1	14	16	36	35
10. Partick Thistle	38	12	5	2	47	22	0	5	14	17	50	34
11. Arbroath	38	6	6	7	22	24	5	5	9	24	45	33
12. Dundee	38	9	5	5	42	34	2	5	12	25	46	32
13. Queen's Park	38	8	6	5	36	25	3	4	12	22	50	32
14. Dunfermline Athletic	38	6	6	7	31	36	6	2	11	36	56	32
15. Queen of the South	38	9	6	4	34	26	2	3	14	20	46	31
16. Albion Rovers	38	8	2	9	41	33	5	2	12	28	59	30
17. Hibernian	38	7	3	9	29	31	4	4	11	27	51	29
18. Clyde	38	10	1	8	35	33	0	7	12	28	51	28
19. Airdrieonians	38	8	4	7	44	37	1	5	13	24	54	27
20. Ayr United	38	5	2	9	30	31	3	1	15	23	67	25

Falkirk and St Mirren promoted.

Did You Know That?
Celtic dropped just three points at home, their best record for 14 years.

🎵 THE FIELDS OF ATHENRY 🎵

By a lonely prison wall
I heard a young girl calling
Micheal they are taking you away
For you stole Trevelyn's corn
So the young might see the morn.
Now a prison ship lies waiting in the bay.

Chorus
Low lie the Fields of Athenry
Where once we watched the small free birds fly.
Our love was on the wing we had dreams and songs to sing
It's so lonely 'round the Fields of Athenry.

By a lonely prison wall
I heard a young man calling
Nothing matter Mary when you're free,
Against the Famine and the Crown
I rebelled they ran me down
Now you must raise our child with dignity.

Chorus

By a lonely harbour wall
She watched the last star falling
As that prison ship sailed out against the sky
Sure she'll wait and hope and pray
For her love in Botany Bay
It's so lonely 'round the Fields of Athenry.

Chorus

🎵 CELTIC'S FIRST SCOTLAND CAPTAIN 🎵

James McLaren became the first Celtic player to captain Scotland when he led his country to a 3–2 win over England on 13 April 1889 in the Home International championship. McLaren scored in the game, which was his second as Scotland captain. He had previously captained his country on his international debut a year earlier, when he was at Hibernian. In total, McLaren captained Scotland three times – his only caps – with a record of two wins and one draw.

❧ WILLIE FERNIE ❧

William "Willie" Fernie was born in Kinglassie, a mining village in Fife, in 1928. He began his football education with a local juvenile side called Leslie Hearts and was carried off with a broken jaw in the 1948 Scottish Juvenile Cup final played at Easter Road. However, his performance up until the time he had been forced to leave the pitch was good enough to convince a Celtic scout to visit him in hospital, and shortly after the visit, he signed for Celtic.

After a few years in the reserve side – and after being farmed out on occasion to the Kinglassie Colliery side – Fernie made his debut at Love Street, Paisley, at the end of the 1949–50 season. In May 1950, he won his first medal with Celtic, a Glasgow Charity Cup medal after beating Rangers in the final. However, Willie was astute enough to know that his overall game was not quite good enough to earn him a regular place in Celtic's first XI and so he worked hard at improving. By the time the 1952–53 season arrived, he was a regular in the starting line-up, although his form was often as sporadic as that of the rest of the team at that time. However, the Celtic manager Jimmy McGrory always had the belief that Willie would make it as a player and his lucky break came when Charlie Tully was injured just prior to the 1953 Coronation Cup final. Willie was called up to play for Celtic in the final. Celtic won and Willie's career really took off.

In 1953–54, he helped Celtic win the league and cup Double and was indisputably the best player in the side. He played at inside-right and, although he only scored 13 goals, it was the quantity that he set up for his team-mates that was so impressive. At the end of the 1953–54 season, he won the first of his 12 Scottish caps and was a member of Scotland's disastrous 1954 World Cup finals squad. Willie was a member of the Celtic side that lost the Scottish Cup final in 1955 and again in 1956. In late 1956, he inspired Celtic to their first-ever Scottish League Cup final victory and then, the following year and now playing at right-half and as part of the immortal half-back line of Fernie, Evans and Peacock, played his glorious part in the 7–1 thrashing of Rangers, scoring the seventh goal with a penalty kick. On 1 December 1958, Willie was sold to Middlesbrough to help pay for new floodlights at Celtic Park. However, in October 1960, he was brought back to help inspire a young Celtic side and responded, leading them to the 1961 Scottish Cup final, only to lose to Dunfermline Athletic. During the autumn of 1961, Willie left Celtic for a second time and joined St Mirren.

Did You Know That?
Willie Fernie was often referred to as Scotland's Stanley Matthews.

❧ STRACHAN'S FEELING BLUE ❧

Neil Lennon[†] and Alan Thompson were both sent off by referee Stuart Dougal in Celtic's 3–1 loss to Rangers at Ibrox on 20 August 2005 in what was new manager Gordon Strachan's first Old Firm Derby game.

❧ THE O'NEILL GLORY YEARS ❧

Following Celtic's 1–0 win over Dundee United at Hampden Park in the Scottish Cup final in 2005, Martin O'Neill left Celtic for personal reasons. Martin took charge of Celtic in 2000 and, during his five years in charge, Celtic won seven trophies:

2000–01	SPL winners, CIS Cup winners, Scottish Cup winners
2001–02	SPL winners
2002–03	UEFA Cup runners-up
2003–04	SPL winners, Scottish Cup winners
2004–05	Scottish Cup winners

❧ CELTIC HELP RANGERS OUT ❧

Rangers were crowned European Cup-Winners' Cup winners in 1972 even though they had lost the 1971 Scottish FA Cup final to Celtic, the Scottish First Division champions, after a replay. Rangers had only been admitted to the competition because Celtic opted to play in the more prestigious European Cup competition.

❧ BELLAMY RACIAL ABUSE CASE ❧

On 9 September 2005 at Glasgow Sheriff Court, a Hearts fan was convicted of racially abusing former Celtic player Craig Bellamy. The fan racially abused Bellamy midway through the game after Celtic had been awarded a corner. As Bellamy went to take it, the fan called him a "wee little Welsh bastard" and was removed and arrested by the police who were patrolling the perimeter of the pitch. Sheriff John Baird said: "This unquestionably justifies flagrant behaviour. There is no doubt being Welsh is part of a racial group. If you commit an offence and show malice to that group then that justifies that the breach of the peace was racially aggravated." He convicted the fan and fined him £250. Celtic lost the game 2–0 at Celtic Park on 2 April 2005.

[†] Neil Lennon actually received his marching orders when the 90 minutes were already up.

⚜ OUR BHOYS HAVE WON THE CUP (5) ⚜

This Scottish Cup final is ranked as one of the greatest finals of all time and had the highest attendance for a Scottish Cup final. The black and golds of Aberdeen played well and brought a huge following with them, but it was Celtic who won the day with goals from Crum and Buchan. The game was played against the backdrop of the Spanish Civil War with placards all over Glasgow urging young men to join the International Brigades.

SCOTTISH FA CUP FINAL 1937
24 APRIL 1937, HAMPDEN PARK, GLASGOW
Celtic (1) 2   v   **Aberdeen** (1) 1
(Crum, Buchan)   (Armstrong)
Att. 146,433
Celtic: Kennaway, Hogg, Morrison, Geatons, Lyon, Paterson, Delaney, Buchan, McGrory, Crum, Murphy.

⚜ THE BHOYS ARE BACK IN TOWN (6) ⚜

"Having spoken to the manager [Gordon Strachan], I thought this is the club for me. I have met one or two of the players, and feel this is where I belong."
***Roy Keane**, on joining Celtic*

⚜ KENNY DALGLISH ⚜

In 1999, Celtic legend Kenny Dalglish returned to Celtic Football Club at the request of Allan McDonald following the departure of Jozef Venglos. Dalglish was brought in as the director of football to assist the new head coach, John Barnes. However, when Barnes' contract was terminated in February 2000, Dalglish filled the void as manager until the end of the 1999–2000 season, winning the League Cup in between. When Martin O'Neill was appointed as Celtic's new manager in July 2000, the board allowed Kenny to leave when they decided that the club no longer required a director of football.

Did You Know That?
Kenny was actually a Rangers fan as a child, and when the Celtic scout called to his parents' house to ask if he would sign for them, the young Dalglish took down all of his Rangers posters from his bedroom wall!

❧ CELTIC'S FIRST WORLD AMBASSADOR ☙

Jozef Venglos, Celtic manager from 1998 to 1999, has been selected by FIFA on various occasions to lecture at the FIFA Academies throughout the world in countries including Bangladesh, Bermuda, China, Cyprus, Holland, Iraq, Malta, Malaysia, Mauritius, Nepal, South Korea and Thailand.

❧ LAST-GASP LOSERS ☙

On the final day of the 2004–05 season, Celtic were pipped to the Scottish Premier League title by Rangers. Going into their match at Motherwell, Celtic were two points ahead of Rangers in the table and, things were looking good for Celtic when they took the lead thanks to a Chris Sutton goal. However, two goals in the closing minutes from Scott McDonald earned Motherwell a 2–1 win, which meant that Nacho Novo's goal that gave Rangers a 1–0 win over Hibernian also gave them the league championship by a single point.

❧ THE CELTIC VISITOR CENTRE ☙

The Celtic Visitor Centre is situated at Celtic Park and its visitors can learn all there is to know about the history and heritage of Glasgow Celtic Football Club from its inception in 1888 to the present day.

❧ REFEREES' STRIKE THREAT ☙

Scottish referees considered industrial action in protest at the three-match ban handed out to Celtic captain Neil Lennon after his clash with referee Stuart Dougal in the Old Firm game at Ibrox on 20 August 2005. The 34-year-old former Northern Ireland international was dismissed by Dougal at the end of Celtic's 3–1 defeat by Rangers, but Lennon then aggressively challenged Dougal. The referee, and the newly formed Scottish Senior Referees' Association, expressed their disappointment with the lenient punishment after attending the SFA disciplinary hearing at Hampden Park.

❧ SIX BEFORE CELTIC IN THE LEAGUE CUP ☙

Six teams won the Scottish League Cup before Celtic's first final victory in 1957:

Rangers ❖ East Fife ❖ Motherwell ❖ Dundee ❖ Hearts ❖ Aberdeen

🎽 IRISH INTERNATIONAL CELTIC XI 🎽

1
Pat
BONNER

2
Chris
MORRIS

4
Neil
LENNON

5
Mick
McCARTHY

3
Anton
ROGAN

6
Bertie
PEACOCK

7
Charlie
TULLY

8
Patsy
GALLACHER

10
Charlie
GALLACHER

9
Sean
FALLON

11
Peter
KAVANAGH

Reserves
Allen *McKNIGHT* • Willie *MALEY* • Tommy *COYNE*
Aiden *McGEADY* • Joe *HAVERTY*
Manager
Martin *O'NEILL*

Did You Know That?
Willie Maley was the first Irish-born manager of Celtic.

🎽 JAKE MADDEN 🎽

Celtic's John "Jake" Madden holds the club record for the greatest number of goals scored for Scotland in relation to the number of games played. Jake scored four times for Scotland against Wales on 18 March 1893 in an 8–0 win and he scored again versus Wales in a 2–2 draw on 23 March 1895. They were his only two international appearances.

🎽 AN UNHAPPY NEW YEAR'S DAY 🎽

On New Year's Day 1963, Celtic lost 0–4 to Rangers at Ibrox, a result that kept Rangers on top of the league, a point ahead of Partick Thistle. This was the year of the great freeze, with the weather playing havoc with fixtures. The first round of the Scottish Cup, due to take place on 12 January, wasn't completed until 11 March.

🎇 SPROULE WREAKS HAVOC 🎇

On 30 April 2005, Ivan Sproule scored his first goal for Hibs during the Easter Road club's shock 3–1 win – a defeat that contributed to Celtic losing the league to Rangers. Four months later, on 27 August 2005, Sproule came on as a substitute against Rangers and scored a hat-trick in Hibs' 3–0 win, the first by a Hibs player at Ibrox in 103 years.

🎇 STEIN TRIBUTE 🎇

Prior to their Scottish League game against Aberdeen at Celtic Park on 10 September 2005, the Celtic fans and the club held a massive celebration of the life of Jock Stein[†]. A number of the Lisbon Lions walked onto the pitch and set the European Cup down in the centre circle and, as images of the Great Man in his heyday flashed up on the big screen, a minute's applause was enjoyed by all in attendance. The Aberdeen fans, to their credit, also joined in, holding aloft a banner in the Big Man's memory. Twenty years earlier, on 10 September 1985, Scotland played a World Cup qualifying match against Wales in Cardiff. After going a goal behind, Scotland got a late equalizer to earn a 1–1 draw. The draw gave Scotland the single point they needed to reach the 1986 finals in Mexico. As the final whistle sounded, with the players celebrating on the pitch and the fans jumping for joy on the terraces, Jock Stein collapsed and died. During Jock Stein's era of unprecedented triumph, Aberdeen had always given Celtic a run for their money. Eddie Turnbull's Aberdeen beat Celtic in the 1970 Scottish Cup final, and Ally MacLeod's Dons beat Celtic in the 1976 Scottish League Cup final. However, this day truly belonged to the "Big Man", as Celtic swept Aberdeen aside 2–0, with goals from Zurawski and Petrov.

🎇 STRACHAN'S BHOYS ROMP HOME 🎇

On 28 August 2005, Celtic, comprising mainly of players purchased by Gordon Strachan, beat Dunfermline Athletic 4–0 at East End Park to climb above Rangers and into second place behind Hearts in the SPL table. Polish international Maciej Zurawski scored twice, his first goals for the club, with John Hartson and Shunsuke Nakamura also on the scoresheet. The 4–0 victory was Gordon Strachan's biggest domestic victory since he became the Celtic manager.

[†] *It was at the suggestion of the Celtic fans that a minute's applause – as opposed to silence – was chosen as a tribute to the Big Man.*

🏵 OUR BHOYS HAVE WON THE CUP (6) 🏵

The Empire Exhibition Trophy in 1938 was a counterblast to Nazi propaganda and was played at a time when people began to realize that a war was inevitable. The final was held at Bellahouston Park, but all the games in the competition between Scotland's and England's finest were played at Ibrox Park. Celtic beat Sunderland and Hearts before going on to beat Everton in the final. The final itself was goalless until Johnny Crum scored in extra time: he celebrated by doing a Highland fling in front of the spectators. This was the closest that any team would come to being nominated the champions of Britain.

EMPIRE EXHIBITION TROPHY 1938

10 JUNE 1938, IBROX PARK, GLASGOW, SCOTLAND
Celtic (0) 1   **v**   **Everton** (0) 0
Att. 80,000
Celtic: Kennaway, Hogg, Morrison, Geatons, Lyon, Paterson, Delaney, MacDonald, Crum, Divers, Murphy.

🏵 CHINESE STAR COMES TO CELTIC PARK 🏵

Du Wei, the Chinese international defender who signed for Celtic on 31 August 2005, revealed that a former Rangers legend had played a significant role in his decision to sign a four-year contract with Celtic. Jorg Albertz, nicknamed "The Hammer", was a championship-winning team-mate of Du Wei two years ago when Shanghai Shenhua won the Chinese league championship. Du Wei said: "I talked to Jorg and he gave me many recommendations about my career. He told me that Scotland is a very nice country and that Glasgow is a great city with very friendly people. He told me that by coming here as a footballer I would have a great opportunity to develop my career and become a better player."

🏵 WHITE FEATHER NEARLY A BHOY 🏵

In May 2002, the media reported that Fabrizio Ravenelli, nicknamed "The White Feather", had stated his desire to join Celtic. Ravanelli was quoted as saying: "I have spoken to my good friend Paolo Di Canio who enjoyed his time at Celtic." The former Juventus, Middlesbrough and Derby County striker who played 22 times for Italy, was said to have been impressed by the club's huge fan base and its state-of-the-art stadium.

✿❧ CELTIC'S 26 CAPS ❧✿

Celtic occupy second place in the table for having had the highest number of players capped by Scotland in a single season for the most number of seasons, with 26 between 1872–73 and 2004–05. Rangers top the table with 50.

✿❧ SCORING INTERNATIONAL DEBUTANTS ❧✿

Up until the end of the 2004–05 season, 12 Celtic players have scored on their international debuts for Scotland. This is the third highest number of players from any club, six behind Rangers and five behind Queen's Park.

✿❧ THE SCOTTISH CUP KINGS ❧✿

The Old Firm has dominated the Scottish Cup with Celtic leading the way with 33 wins to Rangers' 30. Queen's Park are in third place on the list with ten triumphs, although their last was back in 1893. Next up are Aberdeen with seven victories, all recorded after the Second World War, and 2006 winners Hearts, also with seven.

✿❧ AITKEN LAST CAPPED BUDDY ❧✿

Ex-Celtic captain Roy Aitken was the last St Mirren player to win a full international cap for Scotland. Roy came on as a substitute in a Euro '92 qualifier against Romania in Bucharest in October 1991 which Scotland lost 1–0. However, despite the loss, Scotland still went on to win the group. It was Big Roy's 57th and final cap in an international career that spanned 12 seasons. He won 50 caps during his time at Celtic, six with Newcastle United and one from his solitary appearance as a Buddy.

✿❧ THE MAGIC MAN ❧✿

Celtic's Polish international striker Maciej Zurawski is affectionately nicknamed "Magic" by the Celtic faithful. Prior to joining Celtic in July 2005, he won four Polish Championships, one Polish Cup and one Polish League Cup with Wisla Krakow[†]. He was also Poland's top goalscorer in seasons 2001–02 and 2003–04. In February 2006, Magic was named the SPL Player of the Month.

[†]*Wisla Krakow was known as Gwardyjskie Towarzystwo Sportowe Wisla from the end of World War II up to 1990.*

❧ JIMMY JOHNSTONE ❧

Jimmy Johnstone was born in Viewpark, near Uddingston, on 30 September 1944. He was born into a very Celtic-minded family and, by 1958, had become a ballboy at Celtic Park before joining them as a player in November 1961. As a young boy, Jimmy constantly practised his footballing skills, inspired by the great Stanley Matthews of Blackpool and England.

He made his Celtic debut in an appalling 0–6 defeat by Kilmarnock on 27 March 1963. On 4 May 1963, he was the best player on the field when Celtic drew the Scottish Cup final with Rangers. He was surprisingly dropped for the replay, which Celtic lost 0–3. By 1964, he was playing well for Celtic in their partial recovery from the early part of the year, but by the time Jock Stein arrived in January 1965, he was out of favour. Although the Johnstone-Stein relationship was not without incident, there is no doubt that the Big Man eventually got the best out of Jimmy and that Jimmy grew to see in Jock a father figure whom he could respect and admire.

European adventures posed a particular problem for Jimmy, as he suffered from a fear of flying. However, the canny Stein often turned Jinky's fear to his advantage and, on one occasion, said that Jimmy would be exempt from a trip to Yugoslavia if Celtic had a substantial lead from the first leg of a European Cup tie. Jimmy inspired Celtic to a 5–1 lead and he stayed at home as the team drew 1–1 in Belgrade. It was in Europe that he was most revered and the diminutive redhead dribbled his way around many players who were widely regarded as the best defenders in the world.

He may have been afraid of flying, but one thing that he did not lack was courage when facing some of the brutal Spanish or Argentinian defenders he had to encounter. His courage lay in his determination to come back after having been downed, knowing that he might be downed again. Sometimes he would beat the defender ... and then he could not resist beating him again. The crowd loved his showmanship.

Jimmy was one of the few players – Lennox and McNeill being the others – who stayed the course of all nine league titles in a row between 1966 and 1974, and it is his trickery which symbolized a generation of Celtic. He had many outstanding games, particularly against Rangers, and surprisingly scored a large total of his 129 goals with his head. He was less successful for Scotland (23 caps), but scored two fine goals against England in 1966, which gave Scotland a chance in a game that they eventually lost 3–4. His best game for his country came in 1974, in which he played brilliantly in Scotland's 2–0 victory over the Auld Enemy. He left Parkhead in 1975, and went on his travels, at one point teaming up with old team-mate Tommy Gemmell at Dundee, but his best days were behind him. Sadly Jimmy contracted Motor Neurone Disease and lost his brave battle for life on 13 March 2006.

Did You Know That?
Jock Stein asked Jimmy to dribble with the ball in the early stages of the 1967 European Cup final against Inter Milan in order to win over the Portuguese crowd. By the end of the first 15 minutes, the Portuguese were cheering on Celtic.

✿❧ SCOTTISH FOOTBALL'S HALL OF FAME ❧✿

John Cairney's superb book, *A Scottish Football Hall of Fame*, lists Scotland's top 100 internationals. Celtic lead the way with 23 entries, closely followed by Rangers with 21. Here are the Celtic players listed along with their top 100 placing[†]:

James Kelly (7) ✽ Jack Bell (9) ✽ Duke McMahon (10)
Ned Doyle (11) ✽ Jake Madden (13) ✽ Jimmy Quinn (27)
Jimmy McMenemy (28) ✽ Alec McNair (29) ✽ Jimmy McGrory (41)
John Thomson (42) ✽ Jimmy Delaney (48) ✽ Willie Miller (52)
Bobby Evans (59) ✽ Bertie Auld (63) ✽ Bobby Collins (65)
Billy McNeill (77) ✽ Jimmy Johnstone (82) ✽ Bobby Murdoch (83)
Ronnie Simpson (85) ✽ Kenny Dalglish (89) ✽ Danny McGrain (90)
Charlie Nicholas (98) ✽ Paul McStay (99)

✿❧ RANGERS OVERTAKE CELTIC IN EUROPE ❧✿

On 28 August 2005, Rangers leapfrogged Celtic in the European Cup top 100 league table following their victory over the Cypriot side, Anorthosis Famagusta. Celtic started the 2005–06 season in 13th position in the table with 131 points after 20 seasons of European competition. Rangers were also on 131 points following 24 seasons in Europe, but lay 14th in the table, behind Celtic on goal difference. However, following Celtic's 0–5 away loss and 4–0 home win against Artmedia Bratislava in their Champions League qualifier, Rangers managed to move above Celtic after beating the Cypriots home and away. To make matters worse, Rangers became the first Scottish side to progress to the the knock-out stages of the UEFA Champions League.

[†] *Gordon Strachan (Aberdeen, Manchester United, Leeds United) is at number 96 on the list.*

🐝 OUR BHOYS HAVE WON THE CUP (7) 🐝

This game between Celtic and Queen's Park was a match hastily arranged for the day after VE Day. The game finished 1–1 and no arrangements had been made for a replay, so they counted the corners that had been awarded to each side as an indication of who had had exerted the most pressure. Celtic won 3–2 on corners and can rightly claim to have won the first post-war trophy!

VICTORY IN EUROPE CUP 1945
9 MAY 1945, HAMPDEN PARK, GLASGOW, SCOTLAND
Celtic (1) 1   v   **Queen's Park** (1) 1
Celtic won by three corners to two
Att. 29,000
Celtic: Miller, Hogg, P. McDonald, Lynch, Mallan, McPhail, Paton, M. MacDonald, Gallagher, Evans, McLauchlin.

🐝 CELTIC'S GOALKEEPER DIES 🐝

Celtic's goalkeeper, John Thomson, was fatally injured when he dived for the ball at the feet of Sam English in an Old Firm game on 5 September 1931. The collision fractured Thomson's skull and he died shortly afterwards as a result of the injury. Thomson was only 23 years old and had won four caps for Scotland at the time of his death. He was widely regarded as a magnificent goalkeeper, despite being under 5ft 9in. John was a native of Fife and was buried in Cardenden with a reported 30,000 mourners present, many of whom were unemployed and who had walked from Glasgow to Fife. In addition, two special trains carried 2,000 Celtic fans from Glasgow to attend his funeral. Thomson's death also had a traumatic effect on Sam English, who was never the same player afterwards. Sections of fans claimed that his challenge on Thomson had been deliberate, resulting in English being transferred to Liverpool. After a brief spell on Merseyside, he grew disillusioned with football and returned home to his native Ireland.

🐝 THE BHOYS ARE BACK IN TOWN (7) 🐝

"I don't see anything positive about my own performance in the final. Scoring two goals in the final doesn't mean anything if you lose. All I wanted was for Celtic was to win the cup."
***Henrik Larsson**, after the UEFA Cup final defeat against Porto in 2003*

❧ CHRISTMAS CHEER ☙

A full set of Scottish League fixtures last took place on Christmas Day in 1971 and the old First Division saw some high-scoring games, with Celtic beating Hearts 3–2 at Celtic Park.

❧ DUMFRIES TEAM BEAT CELTIC ☙

On 12 August 1933, Queen of the South played their first-ever match in the top flight. They made a dream start to life in the "Big Pond", beating Celtic 3–2.

❧ BHOYS DENY SAINTS ☙

In 1970, Celtic beat St Johnstone 1–0 in the Scottish League Cup final thanks to an early goal from Bertie Auld. This was St Johnstone's first-ever appearance in a major final.

❧ SCOT CAPPED BY IRELAND ☙

Charlie Gallacher, who was born in the Gorbals, was on the books of Kilmarnock Amateurs and Yoker Athletic before signing for Celtic in the 1958–59 season. He played twice for the Republic of Ireland in 1967, in games away to Turkey and at home to Czechoslovakia, just four days before Celtic won the European Cup. Charlie was an understudy to Bertie Auld in that great Celtic side. Gallacher played 171 times for Celtic in first-class competitions (106 league) scoring 32 goals (17 league). At the end of the 1969–70 season, Charlie was released by Celtic and joined Dumbarton, helping "The Sons" win promotion for the first time in 50 years in 1972.

❧ AITKEN WORLD CUP CAPTAIN ☙

Celtic's Roy Aitken captained the Scotland team at the 1990 World Cup finals in Italy.

❧ CELTIC IN SECOND PLACE ☙

Up to the end of the 2005–06 season, taking the three domestic trophies as a whole, Rangers top the success charts having won 106 trophies (51 league, 31 Scottish FA Cup and 24 Scottish League Cup). Celtic have won 86 (40, 33 and 13) with Aberdeen in third position on 16 trophies (four, seven and five).

🎰 OTHER INTERNATIONAL CELTIC XI 🎰

1
Artur
BORUC

2
Johan
MJALLBY

4
Chris
SUTTON

5
Bobo
BALDE

3
Dariusz
WDOWCZYK

6
Didier
AGATHE

7
Stilian
PETROV

8
Alan
THOMPSON

10
Lubomir
MORAVCIK

9
John
HARTSON

11
Henrik
LARSSON

Reserves
Marcus *HEDMAN* • Rudi *VATA* • Johannes *EDVALDSSON*
Harald *BRATTBAKK* • Dariusz *DZIEKANOWSKI*
Manager
Jozef *VENGLOS*

Did You Know That?
John Hartson and Chris Sutton are Celtic's joint most expensive signings at £6 million each.

🎰 THE CELTIC VIEW 🎰

In 1965, Celtic was the first British club to produce their own newspaper, *The Celtic View*.

🎰 THREE CELTS IN FERGUSON'S FIRST GAME 🎰

On 16 October 1985, Alex Ferguson, the Aberdeen manager, took charge of Scotland for the first time in a friendly against East Germany at Hampden Park. The new Scotland boss played three Celtic players: Roy Aitken, Maurice Johnson and Paul McStay. It ended 0–0[†].

[†] *A future Celtic manager, Kenny Dalglish (Liverpool), and two future Rangers managers, Graeme Souness (Sampdoria) and Alex McLeish (Aberdeen), also played in the game.*

❧ FIRST OLD FIRM SCOTTISH CUP FINAL ☙

Rangers won the first-ever Old Firm Scottish Cup final beating
Celtic 3–1 on 17 February 1894. Maley scored for Celtic.[†]

❧ YOGI MAKES EUROPEAN HISTORY ☙

Celtic's John "Yogi" Hughes was the first Scottish player to score a
hat-trick for his club in an away European tie. He scored three times
in Celtic's 5–1 win over FC Basle of Switzerland in September 1963
in a first-round European Cup-Winners' Cup tie. Two years later,
in the same round of the same competition and in the same month,
Bobby Lennox scored a hat-trick in Celtic's 6–0 win over Go Ahead
of Deventer in Holland. During the 1970–71 season, Willie Wallace
scored a hat-trick as Celtic beat the Irish champions Waterford 7–0
in the second round of the European Cup.

❧ HAFFEY'S BLUNDERS ☙

The nine goals Frank Haffey conceded against England at Wembley
in 1961 were, for Celtic fans, not his only blunders between the
posts. During his Celtic career he:

- Put a free-kick into his own net! (February 1962)
- Threw a back-pass between his legs! (March 1963)
- In a Scottish Cup semi-final, fluffed his attempted clearance
  straight to the opposing forward, who scored! (April 1963)

❧ CELTIC WELCOME CLYDEBANK TO SPL ☙

The 1977–78 season was Clydebank's first in the Scottish Premier League.
Celtic beat the newcomers 1–0 at Celtic Park in September 1977.

❧ CELTIC'S PALESTINIAN CONNECTION ☙

During the 2004–05 season, a few Celtic fans were seen waving
the Palestinian national flag at some games. However, when Celtic
visited Rangers for an Old Firm game, the home fans adopted Israel's
national flag, "The Star of David", in direct opposition to the Celtic
fans' allegiance to the Palestinian cause.

*'Seven members of the Celtic team had won winners' medals in the 1892 final, and all but Curren
and Cassidy had played in the side that lost the 1893 final.*

❦ OUR BHOYS HAVE WON THE CUP (8) ❦

St Mungo is the patron saint of Glasgow and, in 1951, Celtic met Aberdeen in the St Mungo Cup final. The trophy was a one-off, pre-season competition to celebrate Glasgow's contribution to the 1951 Festival of Britain. Celtic, the Scottish Cup winners in 1950–51, added another trophy to their cabinet by coming back from being 1–2 down to win 3–2. The problem with this trophy was that it practically disintegrated whenever anyone touched it and it eventually transpired that the Glasgow Corporation had bought it second hand. Investigations proved that the trophy had started life as a prize for a yachting regatta in 1894.

ST MUNGO CUP 1951

1 AUGUST 1951, HAMPDEN PARK, GLASGOW, SCOTLAND
Celtic (1) 3   **v**   **Aberdeen** (2) 2
(Fallon 2, Walsh)   (Yorston, Bogan)
Att. 81,000
Celtic: Hunter, Haughney, Rollo, Evans, Mallan, Baillie, Collins, Walsh, Fallon, Peacock, Tully.

❦ THE BHOYS ARE BACK IN TOWN (8) ❦

"Scottish goalkeepers are supposed to be bad enough, but an Irish 'keeper in Scotland ... I just had to go out and try and prove everyone wrong."
Pat Bonner

❦ TULLY FOR RANGERS ❦

Charlie Tully started his football career with local club Whiterock before joining Belfast Celtic. In 1948, he signed for Celtic for £8,000. Charlie Tully spent periods on loan at Stirling Albion and Rangers before he left Celtic Park in September 1959. However, he never played for the Rangers first XI in any recognized first-class game. Tully was an incredible character. In a cup-tie against Falkirk, he scored directly from a corner kick only for the referee to order the corner to be taken again. Charlie placed the ball at the corner flag and promptly scored from the re-taken corner kick, with the referee allowing the goal to stand. In another game, he accurately bounced a throw-in off the back of a defender's head to win a corner. After leaving Celtic Park, he became the player-manager of Cork Hibs, before going on to manage both Bangor and Portadown. He was only 47 years old when he died in 1971.

✼ NINE PAST HAFFEY ✼

Celtic's Frank Haffey[†] was in goal for Scotland on 15 April 1961 when England beat Scotland 9–3 at Wembley. Scotland's goals were scored by Mackay and Wilson (2), while the match also marked Billy McNeill's international debut. It was only Scotland manager Ian McColl's second game in charge and is Scotland's biggest-ever defeat.

✼ CELTIC'S NON-INTERNATIONAL STAR ✼

John Hodge played for Celtic against Rangers in the second Old Firm Cup final on 22 April 1899, scoring the second goal in Celtic's 2–0 win. He was also in the Celtic side that retained the trophy the following season, beating Queen's Park 4–3 in the final on 15 May 1900. Unbelievably, Hodge was the only member of Celtic's 1900 Scottish Cup-winning side who had not been capped at international level, although he did play twice during the 1899–1900 season for the Scottish League XI – in a 2–2 draw with the English League XI at Crystal Palace (the first time that fixture had been played in London) and a 6–0 win over the Irish League XI at Easter Road.

✼ PACKIE MISSES OUT ON CELTIC RECORD ✼

Pat Bonner played for the Republic of Ireland in the 1994 World Cup finals in the USA without being registered to any club side. Ironically, had Packie still been registered with Celtic, the caps he won in the USA and in the warm-up games immediately before the 1994 finals would have made him Celtic's record international cap holder in place of Paul McStay.

✼ SCOTTISH PREMIER LEAGUE WINNERS ✼

At the beginning of the 1998–99 season, the new Scottish Premier League was established. Celtic have won three of the seven Scottish Premier League championships played for up to the end of the 2004–05 season. They took the prize in 2001, 2002 and 2004[††].

[†]*It is reported that Frank Haffey allowed himself to be photographed in front of Big Ben at 9.15 the same evening of the game. The next morning, his grinning face was plastered all over the papers with Big Ben reading 9–3! Haffey later emigrated to Australia where he became a nightclub singer and the butt of a joke which went as follows: "What's the time? Nine past Haffey."*
[††]*Apart from Celtic and Rangers (four-time winners), no other club has won the Scottish Premier League.*

❧ I PLAYED FOR BOTH ❧

The following players played for both Old Firm sides:

Tom Sinclair	Rangers 1904–06 and Celtic 1906–07
Robert Campbell	Celtic 1905-06 and Rangers 1906–14
Willie Kivlichan	Rangers 1905–07 and Celtic 1907–11
Hugh Shaw	Rangers 1905–06 and Celtic 1906–07
David Taylor	Rangers 1906–11 and Celtic 1918–19 *(guest player)*
Davie McLean	Celtic 1907–09 and Rangers 1918–19
Scott Duncan	Rangers 1913–18 and Celtic 1918–19 *(guest player)*
James Young	Celtic 1917–18 and Rangers 1917–18
Alfie Conn Jr	Rangers 1968–74 and Celtic 1977–79
Mo Johnston	Celtic 1984–87 and Rangers 1989–92

❧ WHY THE "OLD FIRM" ❧

The term "Old Firm" goes back over 100 years. At the beginning of the 20th century, there was a considerable amount of suspicion in Scottish football that Rangers and Celtic, despite their fierce rivalry on the pitch, would act together for their own benefit rather than for the benefit of Scottish football as a whole. Indeed, there was a famous cartoon in the *Scottish Referee*, which used the phrase "the Old Firm" to collectively describe Celtic and Rangers. Even both sets of fans suspected that Celtic and Rangers would sometimes "stage" results to secure extra revenue. One of the main causes for the riot at the 1909 Scottish Cup final replay was the belief by the fans that the clubs had colluded to arrange a second drawn game in order to reap the financial rewards of a third game.

❧ YOUNG PLAYER OF THE YEAR AWARD ❧

The following Celtic young guns received the Scottish PFA Young Player of the Year award[†]:

1981	Charlie Nicholas
1983	Paul McStay
1996	Jackie McNamara
2001	Stilian Petrov
2004	Stephen Pearson

[†]Three future Celtic players have also won the award: Frank McAvennie (St Mirren, 1982), John Collins (Hibernian, 1988) and Phil O'Donnell (Motherwell, 1992 and 1994).

❧ NOTABLE NICKNAMES ❧

Jimmy McGrory	Gentleman Jim
Alec McNair	The Icicle
Jimmy McMenemy	Napoleon
Jimmy Johnstone	Jinky
Pat Bonner	Packie
Bobby Lennox	Fizz Bomb
Henrik Larsson	The Magnificent Seven
Billy McNeill	Caesar
Brian McClair	Choccy
Alan McInally	Rambo
John Hughes	Yogi
Johannes Edvaldsson	Shuggie
Dariusz Dziekanowski	Jackie

❧ EDWARDIAN KINGS ❧

For the first 14 seasons of the 20th century, up to the outbreak of the First World War, the Old Firm dominated Scottish football. During these years, Celtic won the Scottish First Division championship seven times and the Scottish Cup six times. Rangers won the league five times and the cup once. The closest any club came to challenging their monopoly was Hibernian, who recorded one league championship triumph and one Scottish Cup final success, while Hearts managed two Cup final victories. Dundee also offered a challenge to the Old Firm dominance at the end of the Edwardian era, finishing as runners-up twice and recording one victory in the Scottish Cup final.

❧ SCOTLAND'S 50 GREATEST MANAGERS ❧

Jock Stein proudly heads the list of Scotland's top-50 managers in a poll conducted by the *Sunday Herald* in 2003. Here are some other Celtic greats included in the top 50 (their positions in the list are in parentheses): Jock Stein (1), Willie Maley (5), Kenny Dalglish (13), Billy McNeill (21), Gordon Strachan (27), Jimmy McGrory (30), David Hay (35), Tommy Burns (50).

❧ THE LION KING ❧

"John ... you're immortal" were the famous words that Bill Shankly spoke to Jock Stein after his Lisbon Lions won the 1967 European Cup final.

✿ RETURN OF THE PRODIGAL SON ✿

"Keano, there's only one Keano" poured down in a wave of emotion from the four huge stands at Old Trafford on 9 May 2006 before, during and after Roy Keane's Testimonial against his former club, Manchester United. Keano captained Celtic in a goalless first half and then wore the red of United in the second half when a Cristiano Ronaldo goal settled the match for the Red Devils. A bumper crowd of 69,591, a record for a testimonial match, paid tribute to Keane whilst Celtic's 23,000 match ticket allocation was the highest ever away attendance at a game in Britain. Keano, a multi-millionaire, donated an unspecified substantial proportion of the gate receipts to Charity.

✿ THE ICE-CREAM MAN ✿

Jack Charlton, the ex-manager of the Republic of Ireland, nicknamed former Celtic star Tony Cascarino "The Ice-Cream Man".

✿ OLD FIRM LEAGUE CUP FINAL MASSACRE ✿

Celtic thrashed Rangers 7–1 in the 1957 Scottish League Cup final at Hampden Park on 19 October 1957 in front of a crowd of 82,293 spectators. Neilly Mochan scored twice while Sammy Wilson and Willie Fernie with a penalty were the other goalscorers.

✿ JOCK'S TENTH AND LAST TITLE ✿

Celtic won the Scottish championship title in 1976–77, finishing eight points clear of Rangers. It was the tenth and last title won by manager Jock Stein.

✿ SIX TOP-FLIGHT GLASWEGIAN TEAMS ✿

The 1958–59 season was the last time that Glasgow fielded six teams in the top flight. Rangers finished second, Celtic third, Clyde fourth, Partick Thistle sixth, Third Lanark 14th and Queen's Park 18th (last) and relegated.

✿ LARSSON BREAKS HIS LEG ✿

Celtic were knocked out of the 1999–2000 UEFA Cup by Olympique Lyonnais at the second-round stage. Celtic lost both legs 1–0 and, to make matters worse, Henrik Larsson broke his leg in the away match.

🎎 A SHOT AT GLORY 🎎

In 2000, the movie *A Shot at Glory* was made. In it Ally McCoist plays a former Celtic player, Jackie McQuillan, and footage of the movie shows McCoist in his Ibrox glory days with a Celtic shirt super-imposed over his Rangers shirt. Celtic's Didier Agathe played for Rangers in the movie[†].

🎎 THE SCOTTISH FWA AWARD 🎎

The following Celtic heroes received the Scottish Football Writers' Player of the Year award[††]:

1965	Billy McNeill
1967	Ronnie Simpson
1969	Bobby Murdoch
1973	George Connolly
1977	Danny McGrain
1983	Charlie Nicholas
1987	Brian McClair
1988	Paul McStay
1998	Craig Burley
1999	Henrik Larsson
2001	Henrik Larsson
2002	Paul Lambert
2004	Jackie McNamara
2005	John Hartson

🎎 DALGLISH GETS WINNING SEND-OFF 🎎

On 12 November 1986, Kenny Dalglish made his 102nd and final appearance for Scotland in a European Championship qualifying group 7 game against Luxembourg at Hampden Park. Two goals from Davie Cooper and one from Mo Johnston gave Scotland the win in front of 35,078 fans. Mo Johnston's Celtic team-mates, Roy Aitken (captain), Murdo MacLeod and Brian McClair, all started the game for Scotland, while Paul McStay came on as a substitute for Alan Hansen after 46 minutes to win his 18th cap.

[†] *During filming, Ally McCoist wanted Rangers to win the match at the end of the movie and when the producer changed the script the teams were also changed around, making McCoist's part in the movie that of a former Celtic player, which he also wasn't too happy about.*

[††] *Future Celtic manager Gordon Strachan won the award in 1980 when he was at Aberdeen.*

❧ SPL CHAMPIONS ☙

The 1975–76 season saw the start of the new Scottish Premier League that lasted until the end of the 1997–98 season. Celtic won seven of the 23 championships (in 1977, 1979, 1981, 1982, 1986, 1988 and 1998)[†].

❧ CHAMPIONSHIP PLAY-OFF VICTORY ☙

Up until 1920, clubs that finished equal on points played a play-off match to decide the outcome of the Scottish First Division championship. In 1905, Celtic beat Rangers 2–1 in the title play-off decider to claim their fifth title.

❧ JIM HAY ☙

After winning six consecutive league titles with Celtic (1905–10), and three Scottish Cups, Jim Hay joined Newcastle United in 1911. Jim, a classy left-half, cost the Geordies £1,250 and he stayed with them until 1919, when he moved on to Ayr United.

❧ CELTIC'S 62-GAME UNBEATEN RUN ☙

Celtic created the current British record of 62 matches unbeaten from 20 November 1915 until 14 April 1917. During the First World War, the Scottish League took the decision to continue their domestic league games, despite the fact that the English Football League was cancelled for the duration of 1914–19. Most of the Celtic players played an active part in the war, as did the Old Firm managers, William Maley (Celtic) and William Wilton (Rangers), who both did voluntary work at Stobhill Hospital in Glasgow[††].

❧ CELTIC'S DUTCH LESSON ☙

Celtic were dumped out of the 1970–71 European Cup at the quarter-final stage by the eventual winners, Ajax, losing 1–3 over the two legs (0–3 and 1–0). Ajax went on to collect three consecutive European Cups. Celtic had earlier disposed of KPV Kokkola (Finland) in the first round and Waterford United in the second round.

[†] *Apart from Celtic and Rangers (12), only Aberdeen (1980, 1984 and 1985) and Dundee United (1983) have won the Scottish Premier Division.*
[††] *Charles Shaw (goalkeeper) and Joseph Dodds (left-back) played in all 62 games.*

❧ THE BHOYS ARE BACK IN TOWN (9) ☙

"The best place to defend is in the other team's penalty box."
Jock Stein

❧ SCOTTISH LEAGUE CUP SUCCESS ☙

The Old Firm has dominated the Scottish League Cup since its inception in 1947, with Rangers clearly leading Celtic with 24 wins to their archrival's 13. Aberdeen are third on the list with five triumphs.

❧ EUROPEAN CUP MEDAL WINNERS ☙

The following players, all of whom have played for Celtic, won a European Cup-winners' medal during their career:

Ronnie Simpson	Celtic 1967
Jim Craig	Celtic 1967
Tommy Gemmell	Celtic 1967
Bobby Murdoch	Celtic 1967
Billy McNeill	Celtic 1967
John Clark	Celtic 1967
Jimmy Johnstone	Celtic 1967
Willie Wallace	Celtic 1967
Stevie Chalmers	Celtic 1967
Bertie Auld	Celtic 1967
Tommy Lennox	Celtic 1967
Paddy Crerand	Manchester United 1968
Kenny Dalglish	Liverpool 1978, 1981 and 1984
Paul Lambert	Borussia Dortmund 1997
Roy Keane	Manchester United 1999

❧ INTER EXACT THEIR REVENGE ☙

Celtic made it to the semi-finals of the European Cup for the second successive season in 1971–72 in what was their sixth consecutive appearance in the competition. However, the team they had gloriously defeated in the 1967 final, Inter Milan, exacted their revenge with a cruel 5–4 win on penalties after both legs had ended goalless. Celtic had seen off B1903 Copenhagen (Denmark), Sliema Wanderers (Malta) and Ujpest Budapest (Hungary) in the earlier rounds.

❧ HENRIK LARSSON ❧

Henrik Larsson was born on 20 September 1971 in Helsingborg, Sweden, and played for the team of the same name before moving to Feyenoord, winning his first Swedish cap in 1993 and starring in the 1994 World Cup. However, he was more or less a complete unknown in Scotland when Wim Jansen brought him to Celtic in the summer of 1997. His first appearance for the Hoops was distinctly inauspicious, coming on as a substitute at Easter Road and promptly giving the ball away to concede a goal! His first goal in a Celtic shirt was an own-goal in the UEFA Cup, but fortunately, a brilliant goal against St Johnstone shortly afterwards managed to persuade the Celtic faithful that they had a superstar in the making. Henrik's dreadlocks became a feature of the 1997–98 season, as Celtic returned to glory, winning the League Cup in November 1997 and the Premier League championship in May 1998 to deny Rangers their much-craved ten-in-a-row.

However, this success did not last long, as Celtic immediately plunged into self-destructive internecine strife, and the next two seasons were barren ones. Things might just have been different had Henrik not broken his leg in a European game against Lyon in November 1999. However, Celtic's fortunes turned in the summer of 2000 with the arrival of Martin O'Neill and the restoration of Henrik Larsson to full fitness. By October 2000 the dreadlocks had gone, but the skill and the goalscoring had returned. It was a great season and Henrik's admirers were a little disappointed that he did not quite beat McGrory's record of 50 goals (from the 1935–36 season) or score a hat-trick in the Cup final, which would have put him on a par with Quinn and Deans. Songs like "Henrik Larsson is the King of Kings" resounded round Scotland's grounds that season, as well as "The Magnificent Seven" at Parkhead whenever he scored.

During the following seasons Henrik's form remained superb, both for Celtic and for Sweden in the 2002 World Cup finals. He scored twice in Celtic's 2003 UEFA Cup final defeat to Porto, after having recovered from a broken jaw.

Henrik's great goalscoring ability often masked the fact that he was also a magnificent player who possessed an uncanny ability to turn, beat an opponent and find a team-mate with unerring accuracy.

Henrik celebrated a goal with his trademark aeroplane impersonation and he always ran to the crowd so that he could share his joy with them. The latter is possibly why the Celtic fans had so much respect for him. On the pitch he always gave 100 per cent, never seemed to tire and was a model professional with his perpetual energy. Even after he moved to Barcelona, he never lost his zest for the game.

❧ THE CELTIC SONG ❧

Hail Hail, the Celts are here,
What the hell do we care,
What the hell do we care,
Hail Hail, the Celts are here,
What the hell do we care now...

For its a grand old team to play for,
For its a grand old team to see,
And if you know the history,
Its enough to make your heart go,
Nine-in-a-row.

We don't care what the animals say,
What the hell do we care,
For we only know,
That there's gonna be a show,
And the Glasgow Celtic will be there.

Sure it's the best darn team in Scotland
And the players they are grand,
"We support the Celtic"
'Cos they are the finest in the land.
We'll be there to give the Bhoys a cheer
When the league flag flies,
And the cheers go up 'cos we know the Scottish Cup
Is coming home to rest at Paradise.

❧ THE QUALITY STREET GANG ❧

The Celtic reserve team in the late 1960s was so good that it was nicknamed "The Quality Street Gang"[†]. It included future Celtic legends such as Kenny Dalglish, Danny McGrain, David Hay and Lou Macari.

❧ 17-UP ❧

On their way to clinching their 17th Scottish First Division title in the 1925–26 season, Celtic beat Cowdenbeath 6–1 at Celtic Park.

[†] *During the 1960s and 1970s in Manchester, the Quality Street Gang were the main perpetrators of organized crime in the city.*

🕸 WE ARE THE CHAMPIONS (6) 🕸

The 1953–54 season saw Celtic win the Double for the first time since 1913–14. It was by no means a great Celtic side, but it was a more than adequate one, with fine players like Evans, Fernie and Tully all at their peak. However, the one player who deserves the most credit for the Double feat was the captain, Jock Stein, who, although he admitted that he was not a great player, was nevertheless a great leader and inspired the rest of the team. The league championship was clinched at Easter Road on 17 April, and Celtic went on to win the cup exactly one week later, against Aberdeen.

Scottish League 1953–54
"A" Division

| | P | | Home | | | | | Away | | | | Pts |
		W	D	L	F	A	W	D	L	F	A	
1. Celtic	30	14	1	0	40	7	6	2	7	32	22	43
2. Heart of Midlothian	30	9	3	3	42	24	7	3	5	28	21	38
3. Partick Thistle	30	9	0	6	42	22	8	1	6	34	32	35
4. Rangers	30	9	4	2	35	11	4	4	7	21	24	34
5. Hibernian	30	9	1	5	38	18	6	3	6	34	33	34
6. East Fife	30	11	3	1	37	13	2	5	8	18	32	34
7. Dundee	30	11	3	1	31	12	3	3	9	15	35	34
8. Clyde	30	8	1	6	36	36	7	3	5	28	31	34
9. Aberdeen	30	10	2	3	34	14	5	1	9	32	37	33
10. Queen of the South	30	10	2	3	50	28	4	2	9	22	30	32
11. St Mirren	30	7	3	5	27	22	5	1	9	17	32	28
12. Raith Rovers	30	7	3	5	37	21	3	3	9	19	39	26
13. Falkirk	30	5	5	5	31	31	4	2	9	16	30	25
14. Stirling Albion	30	8	1	6	27	21	2	3	10	12	41	24
15. Airdrieonians	30	4	5	6	29	35	1	0	14	12	57	15
16. Hamilton Academicals	30	4	1	10	17	35	0	2	13	12	59	11

Motherwell and Kilmarnock promoted.

🕸 CELTIC VISIT THE HOLY LAND 🕸

In the 1999–2000 UEFA Cup, Celtic played Hapoel Tel-Aviv[†] in the first round. Celtic won 2–0 at home and 1–0 away to progress comfortably to the second round.

[†]*The Hapoel Tel-Aviv fans call their bitter rivals, the Maccabi Tel-Aviv fans, "Nazis".*

❧ DAVID HAY ❧

David Hay was appointed as Celtic manager after Billy McNeill left the club in 1983. Hay, a former player, was just 35 years old. David was a likeable, easy-going person who was sometimes seen by the Celtic fans and board as being just a little too laid-back. As a result, the board decided to appoint the fiery Frank Connor as his assistant; it created a good-cop-bad-cop set-up. In his first season in charge, 1983–84, Celtic got off to a flyer in the league, winning their opening five games. However, by the end of the season, Celtic finished as runners-up in the Scottish Premier League and had lost three cup finals at Hampden Park.

The 1984-85 season was Hay's most successful as Celtic manager by far, and included the Scottish FA Cup final victory against Dundee United (2–1). However, the cup success was somewhat overshadowed by the news that the fans' favourite, Frank McGarvey, was leaving Celtic Park. In February 1986, Frank Connor also left the club. All was not doom and gloom, however, as Celtic embarked on an unbeaten run of 16 games: enough to springboard them to the Scottish Premier League title at the end of the 1985–86 season.

With the prospect of European Cup football in the 1986–87 season – 20 years on from Celtic's first and only successful campaign in the competition – Hay was keen to strengthen the team by bringing in new players. However, the board did not agree with his request, with one director saying: "If Davie's going to buy a couple of players, the money will have to come from his own pocket." During the course of that season, Hay landed himself in trouble with the SFA following several outbursts. On one occasion, he lambasted David Syme – the referee in Celtic's Skol Cup final battle against Rangers – for poor decisions.

In May 1987, Hay was replaced by a former manager, Billy McNeill. After leaving Celtic Park, he had a successful period in Norway before returning to Scottish football to take charge of St Mirren. Looking back on his life at Celtic Park, Hay defended his management style: "I was never too demonstrative because I always felt that the traditions of Celtic made that the way to act. It may have been my undoing, because people looked at me and might say I didn't care enough. Nothing could have been further from the truth."

Did You Know That?
In May 1987, Hay refused to resign under pressure from the Celtic board and became the first manager to be officially sacked by the club.

CELTIC XI OF THE 1950s

Reserves
George **HUNTER** • Sean **FALLON** • Jock **STEIN**
Charlie **TULLY** • Bertie **PEACOCK**
Manager
Jimmy **McGRORY**

Did You Know That?
In 1954, Celtic won their first Scottish League Championship since 1938 and their first League and Scottish Cup Double since 1914.

THE BHOYS ARE BACK IN TOWN (10)

"It was about 75 degrees: it would have burned a hole in your head. We didn't even think about that because when we got the ball we wanted to run and skin them."
Jimmy Johnstone, *on the 1967 European Cup final*

CELTIC FARMED OUT

Dunfermline Athletic beat the Lisbon Lions at Celtic Park in the first round of the 1967–68 Scottish Cup. Before the game, Dunfermline's manager, George Farm, was so cocky that he told Dunfermline to print tickets for a replay at East End Park. Dunfermline went on to win the cup that season.

🎵 PFA PLAYER OF THE YEAR AWARD 🎵

At the end of every Scottish football season, the members of the Scottish Professional Footballers' Association vote to decide which one of its members has played the best football during the course of the previous season. The award was first given in 1978 and was given to Rangers' Derek Johnstone. Here is a list of the Celtic players who have received their fellow professionals' accolade:

1980	Davie Provan
1983	Charlie Nicholas
1987	Brian McClair
1988	Paul McStay
1991	Paul Elliot
1997	Paolo Di Canio
1998	Jackie McNamara
1999	Henrik Larsson
2000	Mark Viduka
2001	Henrik Larsson
2004*	Chris Sutton
2005	John Hartson

(*shared with Fernando Ricksen of Rangers)

🎵 LARSSON'S INAUSPICIOUS START 🎵

Henrik Larsson[†] scored his first goal in a Celtic shirt at Celtic Park against Celtic! The Super Swede scored an own goal in Celtic's UEFA Cup qualifying round tie second leg against Tirol Innsbruck on 26 August 1997. Celtic lost the first leg in Austria 2–1, but won the home leg 6–3.

🎵 THE THREE AMIGOS 🎵

Jorge Cadete, Paolo Di Canio and Pierre van Hooijdonk were dubbed "The Three Amigos" by Celtic's managing director Fergus McCann, who found himself at odds with all three players when it came to improved contract negotiations.

[†]Henrik made his Celtic debut on Sunday, 3 August 1997 as a substitute in a 2–1 defeat at Hibernian. Many of the Celtic faithful were probably wondering how long he would last at Celtic, as Henrik's first contribution in a Celtic shirt was to miss-pass the ball about 30 metres out from the Celtic goal and put the ball right into the path of Hibs' (Celtic mad) Chick Charnley, who scored Hibs' second goal with a long-range effort.

❧ OUR BHOYS HAVE WON THE CUP (9) ❧

On 24 April 1954, Celtic met Aberdeen in front of a bumper crowd of 129,926 in the Scottish Cup final at Hampden Park. The final is generally regarded as one of the best Scottish Cup finals of all time. In a game broadcast live on the radio, the key duel was between Jock Stein and Paddy Buckley. Celtic took the lead early in the second half thanks to an own goal and then Buckley equalized for the Dons. However, in the 63rd minute Sean Fallon met a Willie Fernie cross to score a tap-in and give Celtic a 2–1 win. This game confirmed Celtic's ascendancy and secured their first league and cup Double since 1914.

SCOTTISH FA CUP FINAL 1954
24 APRIL 1954, HAMPDEN PARK, GLASGOW
Celtic (0) 2   **v**   **Aberdeen** (0) 1
(Young (o.g.), Fallon)   (Buckley)
Att. 129,926
Celtic: Bonnar, Haughney, Meechan, Evans, Stein, Peacock, Higgins, Fernie, Fallon, Tully, Mochan.

❧ NO SHOW FOR IRISH AT CELTIC PARK ❧

In January 2004, Glasgow city council dismissed the possibility of the Republic of Ireland playing "home" games at Celtic Park for the upcoming 2006 World Cup qualifiers, despite the fact that the Scottish Football Association had stated that they would have had no problem with an arrangement between Celtic and the Football Association of Ireland (FAI). However, the Glasgow city local authority pointed out that the city could not stage two internationals on the same day, given that Scotland play their home matches at Hampden Park. The police authorities were also unwilling to grant the necessary permission, given the volatile sectarian rivalries in the Glasgow area. The SFA had been supportive of the idea, because they had forged close links with the FAI after the two associations had presented a joint bid to host the finals of Euro 2008.

❧ ALL OVER ❧

On 5 April 2006, Gordon Strachan won his second trophy in his first season as manager of Celtic when they beat second-placed Hearts 1–0 at Celtic Park to clinch the 2005–06 Scottish Premier League championship.

✤ SWISS CHUMS ✤

In the 1973–74 season, FC Basle of Switzerland became the first team that Celtic had met in European competition for the third time. Celtic had beaten the Swiss side in the first round of the 1963–64 European Cup-Winners' Cup, had beaten them again at the same stage of the 1969–70 European Cup and beat them again in the 1973–74 season, this time in the quarter-finals of the European Cup.

✤ LARSSON UNATTACHED ✤

After Henrik Larsson left Celtic Park in 2004, he actually played for Sweden at the 2004 European Championships despite the fact that he was not registered with any club side. Larsson did not sign for Barcelona until after the Euro 2004 finals had been played.

✤ GREEN, WHITE AND ORANGE ✤

Prior to Celtic's European Cup semi-final first leg game with Leeds United at Elland Road in 1970, the referee insisted that Celtic play the match in blue socks, as they clashed with the all-white kit of Leeds. However, Celtic had only brought their normal white socks with them and Leeds offered them blue socks. Big Jock told the referee that that there was no way Celtic would be wearing blue. In the end, Celtic wore orange socks owned by Leeds United instead.

✤ "GRANNY RULE" INTERNATIONALS ✤

Celtic's Tommy Coyne, although born in Scotland, played international football for the Republic of Ireland. Unable to get a start in the Scotland team at a time when Scotland was abundant with strikers – Kenny Dalglish, Andy Gray, Ally McCoist, Mo Johnston, Gordon Durie, Charlie Nicholas, Steve Archibald, Mark McGhee, Paul Sturrock, Davie Dodds, Graeme Sharp, Frank McAvennie, Alan McInally etc – Jack Charlton persuaded him to play for the Republic of Ireland as a result of his Irish family background. Charlton fully exploited the rule whereby a player could play for a national side of the same nationality as his grandparents. Two other Scots that played under the so-called "Granny Rule" were Ray Houghton and Bernie Slaven. Coyne played 22 times for Ireland, scoring six goals. Tommy's final appearance for the Emerald Isle came as a substitute against Belgium in a 1998 World Cup play-off game in October 1997, just 16 days short of his 35th birthday.

🕮 CELTIC LOSE TO TEN-MAN MOTHERWELL 🕮

On 27 October 1999, Celtic suffered a shock 1–0 home defeat to
ten-man Motherwell. John Barnes' side were unable to cancel out
Kevin Twaddle's 15th-minute strike, despite Well's Shaun Teale
being sent off for tripping Mark Burchill 11 minutes before the
interval. In the stands at Celtic Park was Ian Wright, following his
transfer from Nottingham Forest.

🕮 CELTIC LOSE TITLE AT CELTIC PARK 🕮

On Sunday, 2 May 1999, Rangers created history by winning
the Scottish Premier League championship at Celtic Park in a
rampaging, fiery Old Firm game that saw the referee, Hugh Dallas,
injured by a coin thrown from the crowd. The match was only 22
seconds old before the first foul was committed, with a second foul
following before the minute was up.

Neil McCann, who scored the goal that separated the two teams
at the interval, added another in the second half as Rangers romped
to a 3–0 victory over their archrivals to record a first championship-
clinching win at Celtic Park. Jorg Albertz scored Rangers' other goal, a
controversial penalty awarded by Dallas within seconds of being treated
by the paramedics for his head wound. However, the incident which
lit the touch paper for crowd trouble was the sending off of Celtic's
Stephane Mahe, when the home side were already trailing 1–0.

The referee spoke to both teams at half-time, demanding a less
tempestuous second 45 minutes and, although the second half was
played in a calmer atmosphere, two more players were sent off.
Rangers' Rod Wallace was given his marching orders in the final ten
minutes, while Celtic's Vidar Riseth saw red with only 60 seconds of
normal time remaining.

At the final whistle, the Rangers players went to the goal where
the Rangers fans were housed to celebrate, but a barrage of missiles
hastened their retreat to the dressing rooms.

🕮 UPSET BY UJPEST 🕮

Ujpest Budapest, the team Celtic had beaten 3–2 over two legs in
the previous season's European Cup quarter-finals, knocked Celtic
out of the 1972–73 competition in the second round. Celtic won
the first leg at Celtic Park 2–1, but lost the away leg, 3–0. Celtic
had disposed of the Norwegian champions Rosenborg Trondheim in
the first round.

❧ THE CELTIC BOYS' CLUB ❧

The Celtic Boys' Club[†] was founded in 1966 with permission from the late Sir Robert Kelly and Jock Stein. Big Jock took an immediate interest in the club and permitted its members full use of the training facilities at Barrowfield. The club has produced many wonderful players down the years, and the first player to progress all the way through the ranks to the Celtic first team was Andy Ritchie, who would later become Scottish Footballer of the Year. Then came Tommy Burns, from a side that also produced Jim Casey and Jim Murphy. The following season witnessed the arrival of George McCluskey and Peter Mackie into a side that already boasted Roy Aitken and John McCluskey. However, Charlie Nicholas and Paul McStay are undoubtedly the two most talented players to have progressed through the ranks from the Boys' Club to the Celtic first team.

❧ FREE BOOTS ❧

During the 1970s, Celtic's Johannes Edvaldsson, nicknamed "Shuggie", used to get two dozen pairs of football boots of varying sizes sent over from Germany, which he freely distributed among his team-mates.

❧ CELTIC NOT VERY BUDDY ❧

In 1908, St Mirren (The Buddies) reached their first Scottish FA Cup final. However, Celtic were not in a friendly mood, running out 5–2 winners.

❧ ROSSONERI TOO HOT FOR THE BHOYS ❧

Following their disappointing exit in the first round of the previous season's European Cup, Celtic were participating in their third consecutive European Cup campaign in the 1968–69 season. In the first round, Celtic beat the French champions Saint Etienne 4–2 on aggregate and easily brushed aside the Yugoslavian champions Red Star Belgrade, 6–1 on aggregate in the second round. In the quarter-finals, Celtic were up against the best Italy could offer, AC Milan. After a superb 0–0 draw in the magnificent San Siro Stadium in Milan, Celtic lost the return leg 0–1 at Celtic Park.

[†] *David Moyes, the Everton manager, was a member of the Celtic Boys' Club during the late 1970s.*

❧ OUR BHOYS HAVE WON THE CUP (10) ❧

The 1965 Scottish Cup final triumph marked the beginning of Celtic's golden era. However, it all could have ended in tears as Celtic fell behind twice to a great Dunfermline side before equalizing. Then, at the end of a titanic second half, Celtic forced a corner on the left with only nine minutes left on the clock. Charlie Gallacher took it and planted the ball right on the head of captain courageous himself, Billy McNeill, to release an outpouring of joy among the Celtic fans. After the woe of recent seasons, 1965 had been wonderful for the men in green and white.

SCOTTISH FA CUP FINAL 1965
24 APRIL 1965, HAMPDEN PARK, GLASGOW

Celtic (1) 3   v   **Dunfermline Athletic** (2) 2
(Auld 2, McNeill)   (Melrose, McLaughlin)

Celtic won by three corners to two
Att. 108,800

Celtic: Fallon, Young, Gemmell, Murdoch, McNeill, Clark, Chalmers, Gallacher, Hughes, Lennox, Auld.

❧ THE BHOYS ARE BACK IN TOWN (11) ❧

"Celtic Football Club is the fans, without them there is no club."
Paul McStay

❧ CELTIC LOSE BATTLE OF BRITAIN ❧

In the 1965–66 season, Liverpool beat Celtic 2–1 on aggregate in the semi-finals of the European Cup-Winners' Cup. Celtic had earlier disposed of Go Ahead Eagles Deventer (Holland), AGF Aarhus (Denmark) and Dinamo Kiev (Russia) in the previous rounds.

❧ EARLY EXIT FOR EUROPEAN CHAMPIONS ❧

Celtic began the defence of the European Cup in 1967–68 with a difficult tie against the Russian champions Dinamo Kiev. However, Celtic were confident of progressing to the second round as, during their European Cup-Winners' Cup quarter-final encounter only two seasons earlier, they had beaten the Russians 3–0 at Celtic Park and had secured a 1–1 away draw. However, Celtic were not on their game, losing 1–2 at Celtic Park and drawing 1–1 away. There ended Celtic's hopes of successfully defending Europe's premier club trophy.

❧ BUFFALOS OVERRUN BY CELTIC ☙

In the 1984–85 season, Celtic beat KA Gent of Belgium, nicknamed "The Buffalos", 3–1 on aggregate in the first round of the European Cup-Winners' Cup. Celtic won 3–0 at Celtic Park and lost the away leg 0–1 in Gent's Jules Ottenstadion.

❧ CELTIC FALL TO SPANISH GIANTS ☙

Celtic went out of the 1964–65 UEFA Cup campaign, losing 1–3 to Barcelona on aggregate in the second round of the competition. Celtic had already beaten Leixoes Matosinhos (Portugal) 4–1 on aggregate in the first round.

❧ GREEK TRAGEDY ☙

Celtic were unceremoniously dumped out in the first round of the 1974–75 European Cup by the Greek champions Olympiakos Piraeus. It was a disappointing end to Celtic's ninth consecutive appearance in the competition.

❧ CELTIC OUTCLASS FRENCH CHAMPIONS ☙

In the 1968–69 European Cup, Celtic beat the French side Saint Etienne in the first round. Celtic lost 2–0 to "Les Verts" (The Greens), in the Stade Geoffroy-Guichard, but ran out comfortable 4–0 winners in the home leg.[†]

❧ TOMMY GEMMELL'S RECORD ☙

Tommy Gemmell was the first British player to score in two European Cup finals: in 1967 in Celtic's 2–1 win over Inter Milan and in 1970, when Feyenoord beat Celtic 2–1 after extra time.[††]

❧ CELTIC'S HEROES BEAT TEAM OF HEROES ☙

During the 1968-69 European Cup, Celtic defeated the Yugoslavian champions Red Star Belgrade, nicknamed "*delije*", meaning "The Heroes", 6–1 on aggregate in the second round.

[†] *Celtic did not face French opposition in Europe for another 27 seasons; then they lost to Paris Saint-Germain in the European Cup-winners' Cup second round, 1–0 away and 3–0 at home.*
[††] *When Celtic played Feyenoord in the 1970 European Cup final, Wim Jansen – a future Celtic manager – lined up for the Dutch side.*

🏵 THE BIGOT 🏵

During the 1970s, James Barclay wrote a play entitled *The Bigot* which, as well as being very funny, is felt by many to be reflective of modern day life in Glasgow. The play tells the story of a Rangers fanatic, Andra Thomson, and his long-suffering wife, Annie, their children and their friends. Andra's world has two spheres: alcohol and football. The play follows Andra in the lead-up to the Scottish Cup final encounter against Celtic, but his life undergoes a dramatic change prior to the big game. Firstly, his daughter informs him that she is going to marry a Jewish boy called Clarence; secondly, his son, Peter, elects to join the priesthood; and, to top things off, Rangers can only manage a draw with their Old Firm rivals. The play is about Glaswegians laughing at themselves from the inside out and was a huge success. It was quickly followed by *Still A Bigot* and *Always A Bigot*[†].

🏵 CELTIC'S ALL-TIME GREATS 🏵

At a star-studded gala dinner, held on 8 September 2002 in the Clyde Auditorium, Jimmy Johnstone was named the "Greatest Celtic Player Ever". Celtic fans all over the world logged their votes using the club's website. Jimmy's team-mate, Billy McNeill, who led Celtic to European Cup triumph in Lisbon in 1967, was named Celtic's "Greatest-ever Captain" and Jock Stein was voted the "Greatest-ever Celt". Meanwhile, Celtic's 7–1 hammering of Rangers in the 1957 League Cup final won the vote for the "Best Old Firm Game". Super Swede, the "Magnificent Seven" himself, Henrik Larsson, was voted the top foreign player by the fans.

🏵 CELTIC SEE OFF THE LITTLE CELTS 🏵

During the 2002–03 UEFA Cup campaign, Celtic beat Celta Vigo, nicknamed *"Celtiñas"* ("Little Celts"), on the away goals rule. Celtic won 1–0 at Celtic Park and their 2–1 defeat at the Estadio Balaidos was good enough to see them progress to the next round.

🏵 GERMANY'S GREEN PAGES 🏵

Green Pages is a German fanzine dedicated to Celtic and is supported by a website of the same name.

[†] *A number of Rangers fans complained that publicity material issued by the Pavilion Theatre in Glasgow for the play was "bigoted".*

🎇 UNDERTAKERS BURY CELTIC 🎇

Celtic were dumped out of the first round of the European Cup-Winners' Cup in the 1989–90 season by Yugoslav side FK Partizan Belgrade[†], nickamed "Grobari", meaning "The Undertakers".

🎇 HOME FROM HOME 🎇

During the 1984–85 season, Celtic were ordered by UEFA to replay their second-round, second-leg European Cup-Winners' Cup tie against Rapid Vienna at least 20 miles away from Celtic Park. In the original second leg, at Celtic Park on 7 November 1984, a bottle was thrown from the crowd only for a Rapid player to pretend he had been hit by it and UEFA rendered the game void. Celtic won the void game 3–0, a result that would have put them into the third round after they had gone down 1–3 in Vienna two weeks earlier. Celtic played their "home" leg at Manchester United's Old Trafford ground and lost 0–1 on 12 December 1984.

🎇 CHARITABLE BHOYS 🎇

Celtic's proposed charity match against AC Milan in New York on 14 May 2002 was called off because the game would have clashed with the USA's friendly against Jamaica, scheduled for 16 May 2002. Organizers estimated that approximately 80,000 fans would have attended the match, which was to have been held in aid of the victims of the 9/11 atrocities.

🎇 IS THERE ANYBODY OUT THERE? 🎇

The Old Firm game between Celtic and Rangers at Celtic Park on Sunday, 2 May 1999, was the subject of a test by the Scottish Premier League's plans for a worldwide pay-per-listen scheme of SPL games via the Internet. Despite the fact that BBC Radio 5 Live's commentary of the Old Firm clash was available free of charge, SPL director of marketing, Paul Blanchard, said: "We will be putting the commentary of Celtic and Rangers on our website this Sunday evening and are testing it with a view to moving into the pay-per-listen market. We don't view ourselves as in competition with domestic broadcasters as this is basically for an overseas audience." Celtic lost the game 0–3.

[†]*Partizan Belgrade's home stadium was renamed "Stadion Partizana", although it was originally called "Stadion JNA" (Stadium of the Yugoslav People's Army) and seats 32,710 people.*

✺ WE ARE THE CHAMPIONS (7) ✺

Celtic's 1966–67 Scottish League triumph was actually a close run thing, with Celtic needing a draw at Ibrox in the penultimate game to clinch the title. Rangers fought hard and were not a bad side, having reached the final of the European Cup-Winners' Cup, but Celtic always tended to have the edge and, despite losing twice to Dundee United – once at Tannadice on Hogmanay, and again at Parkhead the Wednesday after they had won the Scottish Cup – Celtic somehow managed to keep their noses in front, despite the fact that the fans could see the team taking their foot off the pedal as the European Cup final grew ever nearer.

Scottish League 1966–67
First Division

		Home					Away					
---	P	W	D	L	F	A	W	D	L	F	A	Pts
1. Celtic	34	14	2	1	61	17	12	4	1	50	16	58
2. Rangers	34	13	3	1	54	13	11	4	2	38	18	55
3. Clyde	34	10	2	5	29	20	10	4	3	35	28	46
4. Aberdeen	34	11	3	3	44	17	6	5	6	28	21	42
5. Hibernian	34	10	3	4	43	24	9	1	7	29	25	42
6. Dundee	34	9	5	3	34	16	7	4	6	40	35	41
7. Kilmarnock	34	9	5	3	33	18	7	3	7	26	28	40
8. Dunfermline Athletic	34	9	4	4	46	27	5	6	6	26	25	38
9. Dundee United	34	7	5	5	36	33	7	4	6	32	29	37
10. Motherwell	34	7	6	4	37	26	3	5	9	22	34	31
11. Heart of Midlothian	34	7	6	4	22	16	4	2	11	17	32	30
12. Partick Thistle	34	5	8	5	25	21	4	4	8	24	47	30
13. Airdrieonians	34	7	1	9	27	27	4	5	8	14	26	28
14. Falkirk	34	8	1	8	18	24	3	3	11	15	46	26
15. St Johnstone	34	8	3	6	31	30	2	2	13	22	43	25
16. Stirling Albion	34	3	6	8	18	34	2	3	12	13	51	19
17. St Mirren	34	4	1	12	18	47	0	6	11	7	34	15
18. Ayr United	34	1	4	12	11	37	0	3	14	9	49	9

✺ CELTIC 7 THE BLUE BRAZIL 0 ✺

Celtic recorded their biggest-ever win over Cowdenbeath, nicknamed the "Blue Brazil", in the 1933–34 season, winning 7–0 at Celtic Park.

❧ SCOTLAND'S BEST IN EUROPE ☙

For the 2005–06 season, the Scottish teams that participated in Europe
were seeded for the various tournaments depending on each team's official
UEFA ranking, which is calculated by a third of UEFA's coefficient for
the country and then adding all the points gained by that team – two for
a win, one for a draw – from the first round proper of each competition
over the previous five years. The Scottish teams' rankings and points
totals used for the 2005–06 season were as follows[†]:

Team	Points	Rank
Celtic	63.476	22
Rangers	40.476	48
Hibs	12.476	158
Dundee Utd	10.476	179

❧ CELTIC SUNK BY YELLOW SUBMARINE ☙

Celtic were dumped out of the 2003–04 UEFA Cup by the Spanish
side Villarreal. Celtic drew 1–1 at Celtic Park and lost 2–0 at the
26,000-seater El Madrigal stadium. Villareal's nickname is *"El
submarino Amarillo"* or "The Yellow Submarine".

❧ FIRST ECWC PARTICIPATION ☙

Celtic participated in the European Cup-Winners' Cup for the first
time in the 1963–64 season. After defeating FA Basle (Switzerland)
in the first round, Croatia Zagreb (Yugoslavia) in the second round
and Slovan Bratislava (Czechoslovakia) in the quarter-finals, they
finally succumbed to MTK Budapest (Hungary) in the semi-finals.
Celtic beat the Hungarians 3–0 at Celtic Park, but disappointingly
went down 4–0 in Budapest.

❧ ARBROATH 1 CELTIC 9 ☙

Celtic inflicted Arbroath's heaviest-ever cup loss when they beat the
Red Lichties 9–1 at Gayfield in a Scottish League Cup third round
tie on 25 August 1993. Celtic legend Danny McGrain was the
Arbroath manager at the time.

[†]*Because Scotland secured 11th place in UEFA's rankings at the end of the 2004–05 season, it
guaranteed the Scottish teams two Champions League qualifying places and two UEFA Cup places
for the 2005–06 season.*

❧ BOBBY LENNOX ❧

No player typified the Jock Stein era more than Bobby Lennox. He was lightning quick, possessed tremendous ball control and delivered his passes like an archer hitting the bullseye on a target. He scored 273 goals in 571 appearances – second only to the legendary Jimmy McGrory – in a Celtic career that lasted almost 20 years as a player. When he retired, he then played a great part behind the scenes as a coach at the club. The Celtic fans affectionately nicknamed Bobby Lennox "Buzz Bomb" and "Lemon", the latter in reference to how he made suckers out of defenders.

Bobby was born in Saltcoats, Ayrshire, in 1943 and has the claim of being the Lisbon Lion who was born the furthest away from Parkhead. He joined the club in September 1961 as an 18-year-old and made his debut in March 1962 in a game against league leaders Dundee. He made a few appearances at the start of the 1964–65 season but, as had been the case with Bobby Murdoch, it was the arrival of Jock Stein that revolutionized Lennox. Stein abandoned the idea of left-wingers, moved Bertie Auld to midfield and played Lennox as a "left-sided forward" in a 4-2-4 formation. Lennox came of age on 24 April 1965, when Celtic won the Scottish Cup beating Dunfermline Athletic at Hampden Park in the final

Jock Stein encouraged Lennox to cultivate his speed. Indeed, Bobby's patience was often put to the test when he was flagged for offside by a linesman who could not believe that Bobby could have been that fast. In 1968, he won the Scottish League championship for Celtic when the ball came off his shin as Celtic beat Morton with the last kick. In April 1969, he scored against Rangers in the Scottish Cup final and helped himself to a hat-trick in the League Cup final against Hibs to secure the Treble for Celtic. However, in the midst of all his success with Celtic, Lennox only won ten Scottish caps.

Bobby broke his leg following a collision with Rangers' John Greig at Ibrox in November 1976 and was out of action for a while. However, he refused to blame Greig for his injury and all of Ibrox retained a respect for him, because he always went out of his way to defuse situations that might have led to something serious. He had a short spell in the USA with the Houston Hurricanes in 1978 but, after his old captain Billy McNeill returned to Parkhead as manager, Bobby followed fairly quickly to assist him. He won 11 Scottish League championship-winners' medals, eight Scottish Cup medals, four Scottish League Cups (scoring 63 goals in the competition) and the European Cup with Celtic.

❧ THE BHOYS ARE BACK IN TOWN (12) ☙

"Right through my career I have dreamed of the day I might be offered the job as Celtic manager."
***Billy McNeill**, on being appointed successor to Jock Stein as Celtic manager, May 1978*

❧ FIRST EUROPEAN ADVENTURE ☙

The 1962–63 season saw Celtic enter European competition for the first time in the club's history. They were drawn against Valencia (Spain) in the first round of the UEFA Cup, going out 6–4 on aggregate.

❧ LENNOX SCORES FOR WORLD CHAMPIONS ☙

Bobby Lennox scored one of Scotland's goals as they beat England 3–2 at Wembley on 15 April 1967 and, in doing so, became the first Celtic player ever to score in a match at the famous London stadium. As it was England's first defeat after winning the World Cup in 1966, Scottish fans claimed they were the new world champions.

❧ THE IBROX DISASTER ☙

On 2 January 1971, Celtic were on their way to securing their sixth successive Scottish First Division championship, but still had to play Rangers at Ibrox. At the end of the Old Firm Derby on that fateful day, the steel barriers on Stairway 13 gave way and a total of 66 people were suffocated to death, with dozens more injured in the resulting carnage. It was originally believed that, when Colin Stein scored a dramatic equalizer for Rangers in the final seconds of the game, and just a minute after Jimmy Johnstone had put Celtic 1–0 up, fans who were on their way out of the stadium turned to come back in and ran head-first into a mass of jubilant fans coming in the opposite direction. The inquiry that followed this horrific disaster found this assumption to be completely wrong. What in fact happened was that the crowd had remained to the end and when they were exiting Ibrox Park, a crush happened halfway down Stairway 13.[†]

[†]The game had been played in a very sporting manner, with just two arrests made by the police out of a crowd of 80,000, both for drunkenness. After the disaster, Celtic and Rangers came together to help the victims of the tragedy and a special match between Scotland and a Rangers/Celtic Select XI was played in front of a crowd of 81,405 at Hampden Park.

❧ EUROPEAN NIGHT OF GLORY ❧

So much has been said about Celtic's 1967 European Cup triumph that it is difficult to adequately sum up the achievement. Celtic went behind to Inter Milan, following the award of a dodgy penalty, but then threw everything at the Italians until they eventually cracked. Gemmell and Chalmers were the scorers on this day, undeniably the finest day in the whole of Scottish football's long and proud history. It is also true to say that almost all of Scotland – and a great deal of England as well – was behind Celtic on that day, with many lifelong Rangers supporters happy to share their archrivals' triumph.

EUROPEAN CUP FINAL 1967

25 MAY 1967, ESTADIO DA LUZ, LISBON

Celtic (0) 2   v   **Inter Milan** (1) 1

(Gemmell 63, Chalmers 85)   (Mazzola 8 (pen))

Att. 54,000

Celtic: Simpson, Craig, McNeill, Gemmell, Murdoch, Clark, Johnstone, Wallace, Chalmers, Auld, Lennox.

❧ ALBION ROVERS 1 CELTIC 8 ❧

In the 1938–39 season, Celtic beat Albion Rovers 8–1 away in a Scottish First Division game.

❧ ARE YOU BEING NASTY TO MY BOY? ❧

On 21 February 1914, Celtic visited Forfar Athletic for a Scottish Cup tie. It was the biggest game in the Loons' history, since their conception in 1885. Prior to the kick-off, Willie Maley, Celtic's manager, was overheard telling his players to watch out for a young player on the Forfar team called Eckie Troup. "Sunny" Jim Young, Celtic's captain and a Scottish international, enjoyed earning the wrath of opposition crowds by winding them up and, on several occasions during this particular match, Sunny brought Troup down. However, Sunny, a player instantly recognizable because of his blond hair, always faked innocence and picked up the shaken young Troup, before apologizing to the referee and the Forfar manager, Jim Black, who was acting as club linesman in the game. Celtic spoilt the Loons' big day, winning 5–0. However, although he may have been able to fool the referee for 90 minutes, Sunny Jim was not able to fool Eckie's mother. When the full-time whistle was blown, Mrs Troup chased after the Celtic captain and attempted to hit him over the head with her umbrella.

✪ LION'S MEDALS GONE BUT NOT LOST ✪

On 21 September 2004, ex-Celtic director Willie Haughey paid £44,000 for Lisbon Lion Bobby Murdoch's medal collection at a football memorabilia auction held by Christie's in London. The 28 medals were reluctantly put up for auction after Bobby's widow Kathleen discovered an endowment mortgage deficit. In addition to Bobby's 1967 European Cup-winners' medal (£17,925), Mr Haughey[†] also acquired a silver runners-up medal from the final against Feyenoord in 1970, plus three league championship-winners' medals and four Scottish Cup-winners' medals. Following the auction, Mr Haughey said: "Bobby Murdoch is a Celtic legend and there was a lot of concern that this collection would be broken up and lost forever. I will hand over the medals to the club museum, so that all Celtic fans can enjoy them for years to come. That was the main reason why I was so keen to bid for them."

✪ CELTIC'S SCOTTISH FA CUP UPSETS ✪

Dunfermline Athletic 2 Celtic 0 *26 April 1961*
Charlie Dickson and Davie Thomson scored the goals in the
Scottish Cup final replay.

Celtic 0 Falkirk 1 *23 April 1997*
The Bairns upset Celtic in this semi-final replay.

Celtic 1 Inverness Caledonian Thistle 3 *8 February 2000*[††]
This banana skin at the hands of First Division part-timers Caley
ultimately cost John Barnes his job at Celtic Park.

Inverness Caledonian Thistle 1 Celtic 0 *23 March 2003*
This was Celtic's second cup exit to Caley Thistle in three years.

Clyde 2 Celtic 1 *8 January 2006*
Not only was this the only domestic trophy Celtic failed
to win in the 2005–06 season, but also the Clyde manager
was a former Rangers and England international,
Graham Roberts.

[†]*Mr Haughey already owns the European Cup-winners' medals won by Jimmy Johnstone and Tommy Gemmell, both of which he also donated to the club's museum.*
[††]*The morning after the 2000 upset, the following headline appeared in the sports pages of the* Sun *newspaper: "SuperCaleyGoBallisticCelticAreAtrocious".*

❧ CELTIC XI OF THE 1960s ❧

1
Ronnie
SIMPSON

2
Jim
CRAIG

3
Tommy
GEMMELL

4
Bobby
MURDOCH

5
Billy
McNEILL

6
John
CLARK

7
Jimmy
JOHNSTONE

8
Willie
WALLACE

9
Steve
CHALMERS

10
Bertie
AULD

11
Bobby
LENNOX

Reserves
John *FALLON* • Willie *O'NEILL* • John *CUSHLEY*
Charlie *GALLACHER* • John *HUGHES*
Manager
Jock *STEIN*

Did You Know That?
Soon after Jimmy Johnstone's death in March 2006, it was announced that his version of the single "Dirty Old Town" was to be posthumously re-released for charity to mark his passing. The song, which was written by folk singer Ewan McColl in 1949, was recorded as a duet with Simple Minds' lead singer – and Celtic fan – Jim Kerr. The Celtic legend, who died after a long battle with motor neurone disease, orginally recorded the folk classic in 2003 to help raise funds for research into the disease.

❧ YO-YOS BOUNCED ❧

During their all-conquering 1966–67 season, Celtic recorded their highest-ever aggregate score against Stirling Albion, a 7–3 victory at Celtic Park. Stirling Albion have several nicknames: the Binos, the Beanos and the Yo-Yos – the latter term given to them by fans lamenting their habit of being promoted to a higher division one year and of being immediately relegated the next.

❧ ROD STEWART OPENS NEW STAND ☙

On Saturday, 8 August 1995, Rod Stewart officially opened the new North Stand at Celtic Park. However, prior to the friendly against Newcastle United that ended 1–1, council inspectors were still on site on the morning of the game, but were happy with what they saw and gave Celtic the all-important building clearance certificate so that the game could go ahead. Rod was given a free seat for life for performing the opening ceremony. In 1977, Rod had a massive hit with the song "You're In My Heart" in which he makes reference to his love for Celtic:

> *You're an essay in glamour*
> *Please pardon the grammar*
> *But you're every schoolboy's dream*
> *You're Celtic, United, but baby I've decided*
> *You're the best team I've ever seen.*

❧ THERE'S ONLY ONE JOHN PARROTT ☙

On the final day of the 2002–03 season, Ally McCoist played his last professional football game. Ally was in the Kilmarnock side that took on Celtic at Rugby Park. Ally received a standing ovation from the Killie faithful, having helped Kilmarnock to fourth place in the Scottish Premier League. The Celtic fans, on the other hand, sang "There's Only One John Parrott" as Ally left the field, in reference to Ally's opposing team captain on the BBC's *A Question of Sport*.

❧ GOING, GOING, GONE ☙

In October 1994, a collection of medals awarded to Tommy Gemmell were sold at Christie's London for £40,250 in a football memorabilia auction.

❧ CAN I HAVE YOUR ADDRESS PLEASE? ☙

In the 1895–96 season, Celtic beat Partick Thistle in the semi-final of the Glasgow Cup at Celtic Park. After the match, Thistle protested about administrative errors on the Celtic team sheet. Some of the discrepancies were quite minor, such as incomplete details in a number of the players' addresses. This was the third protest that Partick Thistle had made during the season, but it was thrown out in the end because it was so trivial.

🐝 EUROPEAN NIGHT OF HEARTBREAK 🐝

The 1970 European Cup final was the one that Jock Stein got wrong. Not only did he underestimate the opposition following Feyenoord's triumph over Leeds United in the semi-final, but many fans feel that he picked the wrong team and played the wrong formation against a fine Dutch side. Several players let themselves down badly as well, and hardly endeared themselves to the impoverished supporters by announcing a syndicate to help them deal with their money on the day after the final. Yet, it had all looked so good when Gemmell put Celtic ahead in the 31st minute, only for the Scots to lose the final, 2–1 after extra time.

EUROPEAN CUP FINAL 1970

6 MAY 1970, STADIO SAN SIRO, MILAN

Fenyenoord (1) 2   **v**   **Celtic** (1) 1
(Israel 31, Kindvall 117)   (Gemmell 29)

After extra time
Att. 53,000

Feyenoord: Pieters Graafland; Romeijn (Haak), Laseroms, Israël, Van Duivenbode; Hasil, Jansen; Van Hanegem, Wery, Kindvall, Moulijn.

Celtic: Williams; Hay, Brogan, McNeill, Gemmell; Murdoch, Auld (Connelly); Johnstone, Lennox, Wallace, Hughes.

🐝 BRING ON THE BOOZE 🐝

In July 2005, Celtic's Gordon Strachan, along with Rangers' Alex McLeish, and the clubs' respective chief executives, spoke at the official unveiling of the Old Firm's renewed sponsorship deal with Coors Brewers/Carling, an agreement that will be worth £18 million between the two clubs over the next five years. However, cynics may be looking forward to a game when Celtic run out, in their Carling emblazoned tops, to play in a match sponsored by the Scottish Health Education Group after lining up pre-kick-off for a team photo in front of the "Real Fans Don't Drink" advertising hoardings.

🐝 OLD FIRM BEAT HONEST MEN 🐝

In the 2001–02 season, Ayr United finished third in the Scottish First Division, but were knocked out of both cup competitions by the Old Firm. The Honest Men lost their Scottish Cup semi-final to Celtic and the final of the League Cup to Rangers.

❧ LIAM BRADY ❧

On 19 June 1991, Liam Brady became the new manager of Glasgow Celtic Football Club. A star player for Arsenal, Juventus and Sampdoria, Brady's success on the pitch was never matched by his success off it. In his first season in charge, Celtic were put out of the League Cup following a penalty shoot-out defeat to Airdrie and suffered their worst-ever European loss – subsequently beaten by Artmedia Bratislava in 2005–06 – when the Swiss side Xamax Neuchatel beat them 5–1 in the second round of the UEFA Cup. The barren season was all the harder to take when Rangers beat Celtic 1–0 in the Scottish Cup semi-final and then went on to win the Scottish Premier League. Brady had spent almost £6 million on new players during the season without any return.

The 1992–93 and 1993–94 seasons were no better as cries of "Sack the Board" echoed around Celtic Park during the early months of Brady's third season in charge. When Celtic lost 2–1 to St Johnstone on 6 October 1993 – a result that sent them fourth bottom of the league – Brady's position as manager became untenable and he resigned.

Did You Know That?
Liam Brady was the first Celtic manager never to have played for the club.

❧ CELTIC END RANGERS' TREBLE DREAMS ❧

Celtic beat Rangers 1–0 in the 1989 Scottish FA Cup final to end Rangers' hopes of winning the Treble. Joe Miller capitalized on a poor pass-back by Gary Stevens to slide the ball past Chris Woods for the only goal of the game. However, the goal was a controversial one, as the move that led to Miller's goal had begun with a Roy Aitken throw-in, despite the fact that Aitken himself had put the ball out of play. In the second half, Terry Butcher managed to put the ball in the Celtic net, but the effort was disallowed.

❧ SILENCE IS GOLDEN ❧

When Celtic lifted the European Cup on 25 May 1967, The Tremeloes were No. 1 in the British charts with "Silence Is Golden". However, not too many people in Lisbon got to sleep on the night of Celtic's triumph and the city was far from silent as the Celtic fans celebrated into the early hours of the morning … and beyond.

🦃 THE BHOYS ARE BACK IN TOWN (13) 🦃

"The manager has instilled an unbelievable air of confidence in us. He makes you play better and he makes you want to win. He's got an awful will to win and he has really transmitted that to the players." *Paul Lambert, after Celtic's 6–2 victory over Rangers in Martin O'Neill's first Old Firm match as Celtic manager, August 2000*

🦃 A RECORD 23,000 TON 🦃

In 1922, Celtic visited Greenock Morton, nicknamed "Ton", and set the club's record highest home attendance of 23,500.

🦃 CUT THE BOOZE OUT 🦃

When Celtic played Olympique Lyonnais in Lyon in a Champions League game on 10 December 2003, they were forced to remove their "Carling" sponsorship from their shirts because the French government had banned the advertising of alcohol on television. A booze-free Celtic lost 3–2[†].

🦃 CELTIC AMONG THE FIRST 🦃

In March 1890, Renton FC invited 13 other clubs to attend a meeting to discuss the formation of a Scottish league. The clubs invited were Abercorn, Cambuslang, Celtic, Clyde, Cowlairs, Dumbarton, Heart of Midlothian, Queen's Park, Rangers, St Bernard's, St Mirren, Third Lanark, Vale of Leven and, of course, Renton. The Scottish League was inaugurated in April 1890, without Clyde and Queen's Park, who declined to attend the meeting, and St Bernard's, who were not elected.

🦃 THE JAGS' FIRST-EVER WIN OVER CELTIC 🦃

In the first game of the 1892–93 season, a crowd of 2,600 turned up at Partick Thistle's Inchview ground to see the Jags take on Celtic. Partick had advertised the game as being against the Celtic first XI. However, Celtic sent a weakened side to Inchview and still expected to see off the home side easily. Celtic were soundly beaten 5–2, to give Partick Thistle their first-ever win over Celtic.

[†]*Following the rioting on the pitch that spoiled Celtic's 1–0 extra-time triumph over Rangers in the 1980 Scottish FA Cup final, the Scottish Football League banned the consumption of alcohol at all Scottish League football grounds.*

❧ BUMPER CROWD FOR THE BEANOS ❧

On 11 March 1959, Celtic visited Stirling Albion in a Scottish Cup tie and set the Beanos' record highest home attendance of 26,400.

❧ AIRDRIEONIANS 3 CELTIC 7 ❧

In the 1956–57 season, Celtic beat Airdrieonians 7–3 away in a Scottish First Division game.

❧ WASPS STUNG ❧

Celtic have only ever met Alloa Athletic twice in the Scottish First Division. In the 1922–23 season, Celtic collected maximum points from the two fixtures, with a 1–0 home win and a 3–2 away win.

❧ THE JUNGLE'S LAST STAND ❧

On 15 May 1993, Celtic entertained Dundee in the last game of the season. It was an emotional day for the fans in The Jungle[†] because it was the last time that the famous terracing would be used as a standing area for a Celtic league game. The following season would see 5,000 seats installed and, in the 1994–95 season, The Jungle was completely levelled to make way for the "Stadium that Fergus McCann built". Celtic signed off in style, winning 2–0 thanks to goals from Paul McStay and Frank McAvennie.

❧ ACADEMICAL QUAD ❧

In the 1986–87 season, Celtic won all four of their SPL games against Hamilton Academical. They won 8–3 and 4–1 at home and beat The Accies 2–1 and 3–2 away.

❧ CELTIC MEET THE SHIRE ❧

Celtic first met East Stirling in the Scottish First Division during the 1932–33 season. Celtic won both games against "The Shire", triumphing 3–0 at Celtic Park and 3–1 at Firs Park.

[†] *A certificate of attendance was handed out to a total of 16,000 fans that entered The Jungle that day. In an event sponsored by the Evening Times newspaper, 8,300 certificates were given to fans entering The Jungle and the remainder went to those fans entering the Celtic End (West Terracing) via the turnstiles adjacent to The Jungle.*

🏴 WE ARE THE CHAMPIONS (8) 🏴

Celtic's 1976–77 Scottish Double was Jock Stein's last, and it was a curiously low-key affair with attendances at Scottish football matches significantly down on previous seasons. In the League championship, Celtic's two rivals collapsed spectacularly. Rangers' fans had rioted during a friendly game in England, while their manager, Willie Waddell, had publicly stated that the team would now sign Roman Catholics – it all helped contribute to a fall in their attendances. Meanwhile, Aberdeen, who had beaten Celtic in the League Cup final, never recovered from an alleged bribery scandal.

Scottish League 1976–77
Premier Division

| | P | Home | | | | | Away | | | | | Pts |
		W	D	L	F	A	W	D	L	F	A	
1. Celtic	36	13	5	0	44	16	10	4	4	35	23	55
2. Rangers	36	12	4	2	36	16	6	6	6	26	21	46
3. Aberdeen	36	11	4	3	30	18	5	7	6	26	24	43
4. Dundee United	36	8	5	5	26	17	8	4	6	28	28	41
5. Partick Thistle	36	9	5	4	27	24	2	8	8	13	20	35
6. Hibernian	36	4	10	4	14	12	4	8	6	20	23	34
7. Motherwell	36	8	7	3	38	25	2	5	11	19	35	32
8. Ayr United	36	4	5	9	23	36	7	3	8	21	32	30
9. Heart of Midlothian	36	5	6	7	26	28	2	7	9	23	38	7
10. Kilmarnock	36	4	5	9	21	30	0	4	14	11	41	17

St Mirren and Clydebank promoted.

🏴 RAITH ROVERS LARGEST-EVER GATE 🏴

In 1951, Raith Rovers lost 3–2 to Celtic in the Scottish Cup semi-final at Hampden Park in front of a crowd of 84,640, the largest gate for a Raith match. However, in 1995, the Rovers won the Scottish League Cup (Coca-Cola Cup) when they beat Celtic 6–5 on penalties after a 2–2 draw at Ibrox.

🏴 BHOYS FRIGHTENED BY SPIDERS 🏴

During the 1901–02 season, Queen's Park, nicknamed "The Spiders", beat Celtic 2–0 at Hampden Park and drew 1–1 at Celtic Park in the Scottish First Division.

❧ 25th MAY ☙

Zurich fell in Switzerland,
They fell in Glasgow too,
Then the French went down three one each time,
And bid the cup adieu.
The 'Slavs won at home but went down two one,
And the Czechs were sent their way,
And the Celts were bound for Lisbon town,
On the 25th of May.
Twelve thousand loyal Celtic fans,
In bus and train and car,
Travelled eighteen hundred miles to see,
The greatest team by far.
They came to cheer on the boys in green,
And help them win the day,
And beat Inter Milan in Lisbon town,
On the 25th of May.
The game was only eight minutes gone,
When Inter Milan they scored,
If they tried from then to hard my Bhoys,
They couldn't have scored one more.
And when half-time came with the score the same,
The Celts did not dismay,
They would win the top in Lisbon town,
On the 25th of May.
A goal must come and come it did,
And Gemmell was our man,
Then Chalmers scored and the Celtic roar,
Was heard by gay Milan.
There's been battles won by our Celtic sons,
But they showed the world the way,
When they beat Milan in Lisbon town,
On the 25th of May.
So here's to Simpson, Clark and Craig,
To Johnstone and McNeill,
To Chalmers, Wallace and Lennox, Auld,
For they refused to yield.
And here's to Murdoch and Gemmell too,
To Stein who showed the way,
To the greatest team who showed the world,
On the 25th of May.
On the 25th of May.

❧ JIMMY McGRORY ☙

James Edward "Jimmy" McGrory was born on 26 April 1904 and is widely regarded as one of the greatest Celtic players of all time and certainly as their most lethal goalscorer. He joined Celtic from St Roch's in 1922, but went on loan to Clydebank for the 1923–24 season. Between 1922 and 1937 he scored 410 league goals in 408 league appearances for Celtic (as well as 13 goals when he was on loan to Clydebank), making him the most prolific scorer in the history of British football. In total, he scored 550 goals in first-class matches, many of them with his head, to make him Celtic's all-time leading marksman.

The McGrory family of the Garngad were exactly the kind of family that Brother Walfrid would have had in mind when he founded his football team. The harsh life, which got even harsher as a result of the First World War, was made almost impossible for the McGrory family in 1916 when their mother died, leaving Jimmy's father – himself a sick man – to bring up seven children on his own. Thankfully, the young Jimmy could play football and he soon found himself a place in the St Roch's junior team, earning an extra £2 per week, which was a godsend to the family's finances. His goalscoring exploits soon attracted the attention of the Celtic manager Willie Maley and, in 1922, McGrory found himself at Celtic Park. He made his Celtic debut against Third Lanark at Cathkin Park in 1923, but was then farmed out to Clydebank for the 1923–24 season. Prior to the end of that season Jimmy won his first medal with Celtic, when Maley recalled him to play in the Charity Cup, beating Rangers in the final.

The departure of Joe Cassidy to Bolton Wanderers in 1924 opened the door at Celtic for Jimmy, but he was dealt a sad blow in August 1924 when his father died. The game that really made him a Celtic legend was the 1925 Scottish Cup final, when he headed the winner against Dundee. On 14 January 1928, he scored eight in a game against Dunfermline and it was very seldom that McGrory played without scoring at least a goal per game.

Maley tried to sell him to Arsenal in 1928 to pay for the new stand, but McGrory simply refused to go from the team that he loved so much. Despite his success with Celtic, he only won seven caps for Scotland and on the two occasions when he played against England at Hampden he scored and Scotland won! He was the top goalscorer in the Scottish League in 1927, 1928 and 1936. His best year came in 1936, when he scored a record 50 goals to secure Celtic the league title – there were only three games in which he played that season in which he did not score!

After he left Celtic in 1937, he joined Kilmarnock as manager before returning to Celtic Park, in the same role, in 1945, Jimmy held the position until Jock Stein took over as manager in January 1965. He died on 20 October 1982.

Did You Know That?
Jimmy attended his father's funeral on the morning of 30 August 1924 and then played against Falkirk at Brockville in the afternoon, scoring once in Celtic's 2–1 victory.

❧ THE FIRST OLD FIRM SPONSORS ❧

CR Smith, the Dunfermline-based home improvements company, was the first company to sponsor both Celtic and Rangers at the same time. In 1984, both Old Firm teams displayed the "CR Smith" logo on the front of their shirts.[†]

❧ ALL CABLED-UP ❧

Between the 1999–2000 and the 2002–03 seasons, ntl, the cable TV operator, sponsored both Old Firm clubs.

❧ CELTIC 9 RAITH ROVERS 1 ❧

During Celtic's 1969–70 championship-winning season, they beat Raith Rovers 2–0 at Stark's Park and, in the corresponding league fixture at Celtic Park, the Rovers were soundly beaten 7–1. Celtic finished the season with 96 goals to their credit, 29 more than any other team in the division. It proved to be a very difficult season for Raith, who were relegated along with Partick Thistle after winning just five games.

❧ CHARLES SHAW, MR DEPENDABLE ❧

Charles Shaw was the Celtic goalkeeper in every one of the 62 league games of their British record-making unbeaten run between 20 November 1915 and 14 April 1917. Shaw also played for Port Glasgow Athletic, Queens Park Rangers, Clyde and New Bedford FC (USA).[††]

[†] *Brewers Carling have also simultaneously sponsored both of the Old Firm clubs.*
[††] *The only other player to have played in all 62 games for Celtic during their unbeaten run was Joseph Dodds.*

❧ CELTIC XI OF THE 1970s ❧

Reserves
Peter *LATCHFORD* • George *CONNELLY* • Paul *WILSON*
Dixie *DEANS* • Harry *HOOD*
Manager
Billy *McNEILL*

Did You Know That?
In 1975, Billy McNeill retired from playing football after his 486th appearance for Celtic, a club record. He made his debut in 1957.

❧ UEFA CUP RECORD ❧

Celtic hold the Scottish record for the most consecutive appearances in the UEFA Cup. They played in the competition eight seasons in a row, from 1996–97 to 2003–04.

❧ HAT-TRICK SCORERS FOR SCOTLAND ❧

Only four Celtic players have ever scored a hat-trick for Scotland:

Jimmy Quinn	v. Ireland	14 March 1908 (4 goals)
Duke McMahon	v. Ireland	23 February 1901 (4 goals)
Jake Madden	v. Wales	18 March 1893 (4 goals)
William Groves	v. Ireland	9 March 1889 (3 goals)

CELTIC SET PARS RECORD ATTENDANCE

In 1968, Celtic visited East End Park and set Dunfermline Athletic's highest home attendance of 27,816.

THE MOST EXPENSIVE PAR

On 4 October 1995, Celtic paid Dunfermline Athletic £650,000 for the services of Jackie McNamara. It was the highest transfer fee ever received by the Pars.

CELTIC MOVE THREE CUPS AHEAD

In 1951, Celtic won the Scottish FA Cup for the 16th time, beating Motherwell 1–0 at Hampden Park in the final. Celtic now had 16 wins in the competition to Rangers' 13.

RECORD NUMBER IN LOVE STREET

On 7 March 1925, Celtic visited Love Street and set the Buddies' highest home attendance of 47,438.

CELTIC PARK'S LOWEST GATE

On 24 April 1984, just 4,956 fans turned up to Celtic Park to watch the game against Dundee.

SCOTTISH OWN-GOAL BLUNDERS

The following Celtic players have all scored an own goal while playing for Scotland:

Name	Opponent	Date	Result
Tommy Gemmell	Russia	10 May 1967	lost 0–2
Tom Boyd	Brazil	10 June 1998	lost 1–2
David Marshall	Hungary	18 August 2004	lost 0–3

RECORD CUP MEDALS HAUL

Bobby Lennox won a record eight Scottish Cup medals with Celtic, beating the seven that had been won by Jimmy McMenemy and Billy McNeill. However, the latter two started in all of their finals, whereas Bobby was used as a sub in three of his.

❦ OUR BHOYS HAVE WON THE CUP (11) ❧

The 1977 Scottish Cup final was the first to be televised live since the 1950s, and was a poor game settled by an angrily disputed Andy Lynch penalty. The game was played in the rain and was generally a miserable experience for everyone concerned – except, that is, for the delirious Celtic fans. Celtic featured ex-Ranger Alfie Conn among their ranks that day and victory meant that he had won a Scottish Cup medal for each Old Firm side in a final played against the other. The match also saw Kenny Dalglish playing his last important game in a Celtic jersey.

SCOTTISH FA CUP FINAL 1977
7 MAY 1977, HAMPDEN PARK, GLASGOW
Celtic (0) 1   v   **Rangers** (0) 0
(Lynch (pen))

Att. 54,252

Celtic: Latchford, McGrain, Lynch, Stanton, McDonald, Aitken, Dalglish, Edvaldsson, Craig, Conn, Wilson.
Subs: Doyle, Burns (not used).

❦ THE BHOYS ARE BACK IN TOWN (14) ❧

"What else can I say? How many times can I say it? How many times do you want to ask the same thing? How many times do you want to be wrong?"
Martin O'Neill, being asked yet again about returning to manage in the Premiership in October 2003

❦ GOLDEN BOOTS ❧

Although the Golden Boot Award was not presented before 1968, the following Celtic players would have won the award had it been in existence at the time:

Season	Name	Goals
1915–16	James McColl	34
1926–27	Jimmy McGrory	49
1935–36	Jimmy McGrory	50

❦ VOTE FOR BILLY! ❧

Billy McNeill unsuccessfully stood as a candidate for the Scottish Senior Citizens' Unity Party in the 2003 elections to the Scottish parliament.

❧ LOU MACARI ☙

When former hero, Lou Macari, was appointed as manager of Celtic following the resignation of Liam Brady in October 1993, Celtic were in serious financial difficulties. Talk of building a new stadium in Cambuslang was repeatedly promised but never delivered and then, on 3 March 1994, the board of directors was informed that the club's £5 million overdraft had been exceeded. On 4 March 1994, Fergus McCann assumed complete control of Glasgow Celtic Football Club before it could be declared bankrupt. To be fair, Macari never inherited too many star players when he took on the job, but he still managed to guide them to fourth place in the league, although this was not good enough to secure the club a European place for the 1994–95 season. It was a rough tenure for Macari both on and off the pitch – including a third-round exit in the Scottish Cup – and some of the players openly expressed their dissatisfaction with "Wee" Lou's apparently heavy-handed management style and his willingness to criticize the players' performances in public. Needless to say Macari did not last long and Celtic found themselves looking for their third new manager in as many years.

❧ LENNOX BREAKS HIS LEG ☙

When Bobby Lennox broke his leg in a tackle with John Greig of Rangers at Ibrox in November 1976, the Rangers captain was one of the first people to visit him in hospital the following day.

❧ SPECIAL AWARD FOR CELTIC FROM UEFA ☙

On 17 December 2005, UEFA, European football's governing body, presented Celtic with a special commemorative plaque in recognition of their European Cup triumph in 1967. The award is part of UEFA's "Champions of Europe" season in 2005–06, marking the 50th anniversary of the prestigious club competition. Lisbon Lion John Clark and chief executive Peter Lavell collected the award on behalf of the club. UEFA also announced that they would be honouring Jock Stein later in the season with a special award at Celtic Park.

❧ CELTIC 8 ABERDEEN 0 ☙

Aberdeen's worst-ever defeat was the 8–0 hammering Celtic gave them at Celtic Park on 30 January 1965 in a Scottish First Division game.

❦ NO. 7 SHIRT TO BE RETIRED ❧

After Henrik Larsson's two-goal farewell to the Celtic fans in the 2004 Scottish Cup final, his team-mate Didier Agathe suggested that the club retire the No. 7 shirt in the Swede's honour.

❦ HARTSON THE CENTURION ❧

On 6 November 2005, John Hartson scored his 100th goal for the Hoops following a comfortable 3–0 away win over Falkirk. The result put Celtic top of the Scottish Premier League. The big Welsh striker scored Celtic's third goal of the game to make it 100 goals for him in 182 appearances for the club. Shaun Maloney and Aiden McGeady were the other goalscorers.

❦ CELTIC SEEDED THANKS TO RANGERS ❧

Celtic were awarded the last seeding, 16th place, for the final qualifying round in the 2002–03 Champions League as a direct result of Rangers' long run in the previous season's UEFA Cup.

❦ CELTIC'S ALL-TIME TOP-TEN MARKSMEN ❧

Counting the league, Scottish FA Cup, Scottish League Cup and European games, the top ten all-time Celtic goalscorers are:

470	Jimmy McGrory
273	Bobby Lennox
235	Henrik Larsson
232	Stevie Chalmers
217	Jimmy Quinn
192	Patsy Gallacher
188	John Hughes
177	Sandy McMahon
168	Jimmy McMenemy
167	Kenny Dalglish

❦ JIMMY McGRORY'S FINAL ❧

After Jimmy McGrory headed the winning goal for Celtic in the 1925 Scottish Cup final at Hampden Park, Willie Maley, Celtic's manager, insisted that young McGrory should hold the Scottish Cup on the charabanc back to Celtic Park that night.

❧ CELTIC'S NO. 1 BRITISH STRIKER ❧

Henrik Larsson is the leading goalscorer in Europe for a British club, having scored 35 times in 58 European games.

❧ OLD FIRM'S TOP MARKSMAN ❧

Rangers' Ally McCoist is the top goalscorer in Old Firm games with 24 in both the league (17) and the Scottish Cup (7). The next closest is Celtic's Sandy McMahon with 19 (15 league and 4 cup).

❧ OLD FIRM LEAGUE CUP FINALS ❧

Year	Result	
1957	Celtic 7–1 Rangers	
1965	Rangers 2–1 Celtic	
1966	Celtic 2–1 Rangers	
1967	Celtic 1–0 Rangers	
1971	Rangers 1–0 Celtic	
1976	Rangers 1–0 Celtic	
1978	Rangers 2–1 Celtic	*aet*
1983	Celtic 2–1 Rangers	
1984	Rangers 3–2 Celtic	*aet*
1987	Rangers 2–1 Celtic	
1991	Rangers 2–1 Celtic	*aet*
2003	Rangers 2–1 Celtic	

❧ THE BIRTH OF THE HAMPDEN ROAR! ❧

The birth of the Hampden Roar was said to have occurred on 1 April 1933, when Celtic's Jimmy McGrory picked up a superb pass from Rangers' Bob McPhail to score a classic goal to help Scotland beat England 2–1. Two weeks later, McGrory made Hampden Park roar again when he scored the winner for Celtic in the Scottish Cup against Motherwell.

❧ AND THEY ALL SANG ❧

And they gave us Simpson, Gemmell and The Bear,
They gave us Caesar, Kenny, Lubo and Pierre
With the greats to wear the green
From O'Neill to big Jock Stein
Stands Henrik Larsson, the man with the dreadlock hair.

✨ THE BHOYS ARE BACK IN TOWN (15) ✨

"I don't think he knew what he was going to do next, so what chance did the opposition have?"
***Tommy Gemmell** on Jimmy Johnstone, 1995*

✨ YOUNG GUN, OLD MASTER ✨

On 25 April 2004, Celtic's Irish youth international striker, Aiden McGeady, stole the limelight from outgoing legend Henrik Larsson with a debut goal at Tynecastle in a 1–1 draw with Hearts.

✨ TWO GARNGAD HEROES ✨

Jimmy McGrory was born on 26 April 1904, ten days after another great Celtic forward had hit the headlines. On 16 April 1904, Jimmy Quinn scored his hat-trick in the 1904 Cup final that propelled him to hero status. The poverty-stricken Garngad area had something to cheer about, but little did they know that Quinn's successor was about to be born.

✨ JINKY SENT OFF ✨

On New Year's Day 1965 at Ibrox, Jimmy Johnstone was repeatedly fouled by Rangers' Tottie Beck and, when he retaliated, sending the Rangers player to the turf, he was sent off. Beck miraculously recovered as soon as Jimmy had disappeared up the tunnel.

✨ JINKY THE BUILDER ✨

At one point, after he gave up football, Jimmy Johnstone was working in the construction industry on a project on Kirkcaldy beach. During his lunch break, he went to the pub of ex-Rangers Willie Johnston, where they swapped stories about old times.

✨ FROM FOOTBALL TO TAXI DRIVING ✨

Willie Fernie is a Celtic legend who, after starring for the side during the 1950s and early 1960s, was appointed as a reserve-team coach at Parkhead under his old friend Jock Stein. Fernie helped develop a number of future Celtic stars, including Dalglish, Hay and McGrain. From 1973 to 1977, Willie managed Kilmarnock, but after his dismissal by "Killie", he gave up football in favour of driving taxis.

🏵 A STAR IS BORN 🏵

It was Henrik Larsson's goal in the first minute of the gut-wrenching last game of the 1997–98 season against St Johnstone that set Celtic on their way to securing the league championship. By now Celtic fans had adopted Henrik as one of their own, claiming (no doubt to Henrik's embarrassment):

He wears dreadlocks
and he hates John Knox,
oh, Henrik Larsson.

🏵 DONS TURN ON THEIR OWN PLAYER 🏵

During an away game at Aberdeen, the Pittodrie crowd howled, not so much in anguish as in mirth, at the sight of the Aberdeen full-back lying helplessly on the ground as Jimmy Johnstone jinked around him. Not being able to do anything about Jinky's mesmerizing dribbling, the player grabbed Jimmy's leg as he ran away from him.

🏵 STAINED-GLASS TRIBUTE 🏵

A church once wanted to have a painting of Jimmy Johnstone in a stained-glass window, but he politely declined their invitation.

🏵 FORMER CELTIC BOYS' CLUB PUPILS 🏵

Roy Aitken ❖ Owen Archdeacon ❖ Jim Beattie ❖ Tom Boyd
Jimmy Boyle ❖ Alan Brazil ❖ Gerry Britton ❖ Kenny Campbell
Jim Casey ❖ Peter Cheney ❖ John Collins ❖ Ronnie Coyle
Danny Crainie ❖ Gerry Creaney ❖ Kenny Dalglish
Raymond Deans ❖ Billy Dolan ❖ Mark Donaghy ❖ Peter Feeney
Steve Fulton ❖ Peter Grant ❖ David Hay ❖ Stevie Kean
David Kenny ❖ Ray Lorimer ❖ Sean McBride ❖ Chris McCart
George McCluskey ❖ John McCluskey ❖ Tommy McEntaggart
Danny McGrain ❖ Dougie McGuire ❖ Jim McInally
Tosh McKinlay ❖ Mark McNally ❖ Paul McStay
Raymond McStay ❖ Willie McStay ❖ Lou Macari ❖ Peter Mackie
Alex Mathie ❖ Joe Miller ❖ Dougie Mills ❖ David Moyes
Jim Murphy ❖ Pat Nevin ❖ Charlie Nicholas ❖ Paul Nicholas
Brian O'Neil ❖ Alex Rae ❖ Mark Reid ❖ Andy Ritchie
Tony Shepherd ❖ Peter Shields ❖ John Traynor ❖ Derek Whyte

🎵 WE ARE THE CHAMPIONS (9) 🎵

They don't come any better than this! Celtic's last game, on Monday, 21 May, was at Parkhead against Rangers. A draw would have given Rangers the initiative and, when Johnny Doyle was sent off and Celtic were trailing 1–0, things did not look good. But "Ten Men Won the League", as Celtic came roaring back, scoring through Aitken, McCluskey, an own goal and Murdo MacLeod. Sadly, the game was neither televised nor covered on the radio – something that says a great deal about both the BBC and STV.

Scottish League 1978–79
Premier Division

	P	*Home*					*Away*					Pts
		W	D	L	F	A	W	D	L	F	A	
1. Celtic	36	13	3	2	32	12	8	3	7	29	25	48
2. Rangers	36	12	5	1	32	10	6	4	8	20	25	45
3. Dundee United	36	12	4	2	33	16	6	4	8	23	21	44
4. Aberdeen	36	9	5	4	39	16	4	9	5	20	20	40
5. Hibernian	36	7	9	2	23	16	5	4	9	21	32	37
6. St Mirren	36	8	3	7	23	20	7	3	8	22	21	36
7. Morton	36	9	4	5	34	23	3	8	7	18	30	36
8. Partick Thistle	36	10	2	6	31	21	3	6	9	11	18	34
9. Heart of Midlothian	36	5	5	8	19	25	3	2	13	20	46	23
10. Motherwell	36	2	5	11	20	38	3	2	13	13	48	17

Dundee and Kilmarnock promoted.

🎵 PITCH DOUBLE BOOKED 🎵

Despite dumping Celtic out of the 2005–06 Scottish Cup, Clyde's preparations for the big game were disrupted slightly when, the day before the game, they turned up at the local sports centre to train on the astro pitch there, only to be told that the pitch had been double booked and that a kids' football match took precedence.

🎵 THE TWO TENORS 🎵

Jimmy Johnstone loved singing and palled about with Bobby Lennox. The two likely lads were once seen getting off the train before a game in Aberdeen, with their arms round each other and singing "Roll Over, Beethoven".

❧ TOMMY BURNS ❧

When Lou Macari left Celtic Park in June 1994, it wasn't long before a successor was found and that man was Celtic old boy Tommy Burns, who duly arrived in July 1994. Tommy had played for Celtic as man and boy for 16 years and, prior to taking over the reigns at Celtic, had been in charge of Kilmarnock. Shortly after he arrived at the club, he brought in Billy Stark from Rugby Park as his assistant. In his first season in charge, Burns restored some glory by winning the Scottish Cup final: the victory over Airdrie was Celtic's first trophy in six years. When he was appointed the new Celtic manager, he could not hide his immense pleasure and pride, saying: "It is a bit like having a dream that you never think is going to become real."

Burns was like a fresh of breath air at Celtic as he set about his task of changing the entire structure of the club. He quickly reorganized the Celtic Boys' Club and the youth team and expanded the club's scouting network. In January 1995, Fergus McCann, who had assumed overall control of the club in 1994, elected to make Glasgow Celtic Football Club a public limited company. The subsequent share issue was the most successful of any British football club. When shares were released in January 1995, it was anticipated that they would raise in the region of £9.4 million; instead they were oversubscribed by £4.4 million. Burns was quick to praise the fans' generosity.

However, Celtic's Scottish Cup win in 1995 was the only trophy won under Tommy Burns' management. Rangers, with all their financial muscle, dominated Scottish football throughout his tenure; reflected in the fact that Celtic had only managed three wins over the Old Firm in their last 15 attempts. When Celtic were embarrassed by Falkirk in the semi-final of the 1997 Scottish Cup, the defeat ultimately brought an end to Tommy Burns' three years at the helm.

Did You Know That?
During his time as manager, Burns signed some wonderfully gifted players, such as Andreas Thom, Pierre van Hooijdonk, Jorge Cadete and the master himself, Paolo di Canio.

❧ SICK NOTE ❧

Jimmy Johnstone once withdrew from a Scotland squad and a picture was taken of him lying in bed with a doctor's sick note!

❦ BILLY McNEILL ❦

Billy McNeill is a Celtic legend whose importance to the club will never be forgotten. His 831 appearances and 23 major medals were all achieved at the defining time in Celtic's illustrious history. What's more, he remains the only man to have managed Celtic twice.

Billy was born on 2 March 1940 in Bellshill and made his debut for Celtic against Clyde in 1958. He immediately attracted the attention of everyone and the disappearance of Bobby Evans allowed him a permanent place at the heart of the Celtic defence from 1960 onwards. However, his experiences in 1961 might have ruined many a lesser man. In April, he received two setbacks. First came his international debut and the infamous 9–3 Wembley debacle against England. Even worse followed when Celtic lost the Scottish Cup final to Jock Stein's Dunfermline Athletic after an agonizing replay. Three-and-a-half barren years followed, with repeated defeats at the hands of Rangers and, in August 1964, he picked up a serious injury. It was at this low point of his career that Billy, Celtic captain since 1963 and now married with children, toyed with the idea of leaving his beloved Celtic for Tottenham Hotspur but, in early 1965, Jock Stein arrived at Celtic Park as manager and Billy soon became Jock's voice on the pitch. And how fitting it was when Billy McNeill rose above the Dunfermline defence to head home Celtic's glorious winner in the 1965 Scottish Cup final. He was also named Scottish Footballer of the Year that season.

Over the next ten years, Billy and Celtic achieved almost unbroken success, with McNeill undeniably becoming Scotland's best defender, despite the fact that he did not get all the Scottish caps that his talent deserved (29). In the quarter-final of the 1967 European Cup, it was a header from Billy that saw Celtic beat Vojvodina and few Celtic fans would argue that the nine league titles in a row could have been achieved without Celtic's very own "King Billy". Billy produced many great performances for Celtic, including scoring in the 1969 Scottish Cup final 4–0 rout of Rangers, his brilliant performance in both games against Leeds United in the 1970 European Cup semi-finals and his goal at Hampden Park in the Dixie Deans Cup final of 1972.

Following Celtic's triumph over Airdrie in the 1975 Scottish Cup final, Billy announced his retirement: he knew exactly the right time to quit as a player. He became manager of Clyde, then Aberdeen and, when Celtic parted company with Jock Stein in 1978, he replaced the Big Man. In his first spell of five seasons, Celtic won a trophy every year, most notably the epic 1979 "Ten men won the league" game against Rangers, but crucially failed to make any impact in Europe.

In 1983, he moved on to manage Manchester City and then Aston Villa, but his heart remained with Celtic. In 1987, he was invited back for the centenary season and Celtic won the Double. The Scottish Cup was won the following season but, in 1991, after two dreadful seasons, Billy left Celtic for the last time.

Did You Know That?
Billy McNeill was nicknamed "Caesar".

🎵 THE BIRTH OF TWO CELTIC LEGENDS 🎵

On a damp grey November day in 1998, Celtic beat Rangers 5–1[†] at Celtic Park during the second league meeting of the Old Firm of the 1998–99 season. After setting up Lubo Moravcik's first goal, Henrik Larsson scored Celtic's third and fourth goals himself in an exhilarating burst of four goals in five minutes just after half-time. Lubo had put Celtic 2–0 up in the 49th minute, then Larsson banged home a header from Phil O'Donnell's left-wing cross on 52 minutes. Larsson's former team-mate at Feyenoord, Giovanni van Bronckhorst, immediately pulled one back for Rangers from a free-kick but, in the 54th minute, Henrik first missed a sitter from Mahe's pull-back, steering the ball wide from ten yards, then seconds later, Simon Donnelly slipped a wonderful through-ball inside Colin Hendry for Larsson to run on to, and despite Hendry's (nicknamed "Braveheart") attempt to shove Larsson off the ball, Henrik kept his balance and deftly flicked the ball past the advancing Niemi to put Celtic in dreamland at 4–1. A fifth Celtic goal came in the last minute, and this time Henrik turned goal-maker, expertly playing in Burchill with a perfectly weighted left-foot pass inside Hendry for the youngster to run on to and drive an angled left-foot shot across Niemi and into the corner of the net. It was the icing on the cake and the game when two Celtic Legends were born – Henrik and Lubo.

🎵 HAT-TRICK HERO 🎵

After Jimmy Delaney scored a hat-trick against Rangers in the 1936 Glasgow Charity Cup final, he was somewhat surprised after the game when the legendary Celtic manager Willie Maley growled at him: "Don't let that go to your head."

[†]*The 5–1 win was Celtic's biggest victory over Rangers since January 1966 – also a 5–1 win – and the biggest winning margin since their 4–0 Scottish Cup final win in 1969.*

🐝 THE BHOYS ARE BACK IN TOWN (16) 🐝

"I used to sleep with the ball. The first thing I'd do every morning was see if it was there. Football was your outlet. You had nothing else."
Jimmy Johnstone, in 1995, on growing up in Viewpark, Uddingston

🐝 STREAKER BRAVES PITTODRIE CHILL 🐝

On Monday, 25 February 2002, a male streaker braved the cold Pittodrie air to entertain the crowd during Celtic's 2–0 Scottish Cup quarter-final win over Aberdeen. He spent the night in a cell and, when he appeared before the Aberdeen Sheriff Court two days later, he wore an Aberdeen shirt as he pleaded guilty to breach of the peace. His drunken antics earned him a lifetime ban from Aberdeen's Pittodrie Stadium and a £250 fine. The streaker claimed he did it all for a bet after having watched a show on television about streakers.

🐝 STRACHAN THE CUP KING 🐝

Celtic manager Gordon Strachan played in the last team to win three consecutive Scottish Cups. He was a member of the Aberdeen side that lifted the cup under Alex Ferguson in 1982, 1983 and 1984.

🐝 KEANO OFF THE MARK 🐝

Following his free transfer from Manchester United to Celtic, Roy Keane scored his first goal for the Hoops in a hard-fought 2–1 win over Falkirk in the SPL on 8 February 2006 at Celtic Park.

🐝 BOOKIES KNOW THE SCORE 🐝

Bookmakers gave football-loving punters a happy 2006 Valentine's Day when they decided to pay out early on those bets placed for Celtic to win the league. It is the first time the bookies have paid out in February, despite three months and 12 games of the season remaining. The day after Celtic's 1–0 Old Firm win at Ibrox on 12 February 2006, Ladbrokes closed their book on the SPL race. With Hearts 13 points behind Celtic in second place, and Rangers a further eight points adrift in third, the Bhoys were made 100–1 odds-on favourites to win their fourth SPL title in six years. Ladbrokes spokesman Robin Hutchison said: "We've seen enough. The SPL title is done and dusted as far as we are concerned."

❧ KILLIE'S CELTIC MEN ☙

Three former Celtic heroes have all managed Kilmarnock during their careers:

Jimmy McGrory 1937–40
Willie Fernie 1973–77
Tommy Burns 1992–94

❧ THE DELANEY CLAN ☙

The legendary Celtic striker Jimmy Delaney's son, Pat, played for Motherwell in the 1960s, and his grandson, John Kennedy, also played for the Hoops.

❧ SUBBED ON HIS CELTIC DEBUT ☙

Celtic's Chinese player, Du Wei, made his Celtic debut in the game that saw Celtic exit the Scottish Cup on 8 January 2006 when they lost 2–1 at Broadwood Stadium to Clyde. Du Wei's Celtic career did not get off to a good start when he gave away a penalty in the first half and was then substituted at half-time.

❧ KEANO MAN OF THE MATCH ☙

When Celtic beat Rangers 1–0 at Ibrox on 12 February 2006, Roy Keane was named Man of the Match for his outstanding display in the heart of Celtic's midfield.

❧ FERNIE NO BUDDY OF CELTIC ☙

In the autumn of 1961, Willie Fernie was offloaded by Celtic for the second time and joined St Mirren. Willie helped the Buddies beat Celtic 3–0 in the 1962 Scottish Cup semi-final. St Mirren lost 2–0 to Rangers in the final.

❧ GLASGOW CUP FIASCO ☙

The Glasgow FA ordered that the 1901–02 Glasgow Cup final between Rangers and Celtic was to be played at Ibrox. When the game ended 2–2 the Glasgow FA ordered that the replay should also be held at Ibrox. Rangers offered to play the replay at a neutral venue and when Celtic disagreed, the Glasgow FA awarded the Cup to Rangers.

❦ WE ARE THE CHAMPIONS (10) ❦

Celtic won the Scottish League championship very comfortably in the 1980–81 season. Up until the turn of the year, Celtic's league form had not been good, but a fine victory on New Year's Day at Kilmarnock heralded the start of an unbeaten run which lasted until the title had been clinched; the form of a young Charlie Nicholas during this period was a sight to behold. Tommy Burns and Davie Provan also made outstanding contributions throughout the season. The championship was clinched at Tannadice on 22 April, with a magnificent 3–2 win.

Scottish League 1980–81
Premier Division

	P	Home					Away					Pts
		W	D	L	F	A	W	D	L	F	A	
1. Celtic	36	12	3	3	47	18	14	1	3	37	19	56
2. Aberdeen	36	11	4	3	39	16	8	7	3	22	10	49
3. Rangers	36	12	3	3	33	10	4	9	5	27	22	44
4. St Mirren	36	9	6	3	28	20	9	2	7	28	27	44
5. Dundee United	36	8	5	5	34	24	9	4	5	32	18	43
6. Partick Thistle	36	6	6	6	17	17	4	4	10	15	31	30
7. Airdrieonians	36	6	5	7	19	25	4	4	10	17	30	29
8. Morton	36	7	2	9	24	28	3	6	9	12	30	28
9. Kilmarnock	36	3	5	10	14	31	2	4	12	9	34	19
10. Heart of Midlothian	36	3	4	11	10	27	3	2	13	17	44	18

Hibernian and Dundee promoted.

❦ JINKY'S EGG ❦

In June 2005, Jimmy Johnstone became the first living person since the time of the Russian Tsars to have a Fabergé Egg designed in his honour. Jinky's decorative trinket was designed by Sarah Fabergé, the granddaughter of Carl Fabergé.

❦ CELTIC BULLY WEE'D ❦

Clyde, nicknamed the Bully Wee, lying fourth from top of the Scottish First Division, unceremoniously dumped Celtic out of the Scottish Cup on 8 January 2006, winning 2–1 at Broadwood Stadium.

❦ CELTIC IN PRINT ❦

Celtic's Paranoia: All in the Mind .... Tom Campbell, Fort Publishing, 2001

Charlie, ... Charlie Nicholas (with Ken Gallagher), Stanley Paul, 1986

Dziekan, ... Slawomir Orzol, 2002

Feed the Bear, ... Roy Aitken (with Alex Cameron), Mainstream, 1987

Fire in My Boots, ... Jimmy Johnstone, Stanley Paul, 1969

For Celtic and Scotland, ... Billy McNeill, Pelham Books, 1966

Former Glories, Future Dreams, ... John C Traynor, Grange Communications, 2000

Full Time, ... Tony Cascarino (with Paul Kimmage), Scribner, 2000

Henrik Larsson: A Season in Paradise, ... Henrik Larsson (with Mark Sylvester), BBC Books, 2001

Heroes are Forever: The Life and Times of Jimmy McGrory, ... John Cairney, Mainstream, 2005

In Sunshine or Shadow, ... Danny McGrain (with Hugh Keevins), John Donald, 1987

James "Dun" Hay (1881–1940), ... Roy Hay, Sports and Editorial Services, 2004

Jinky: Now and Then, ... Jimmy Johnstone, Mainstream, 1988

Jock Stein: The Definitive Biography, ... Archie Macpherson, Highdown, 2004

John Barnes: The Autobiography, ... Headline, 1999

Keep the Faith, ... Ron McKenna and Carlos Alba, Mainstream, 2001

Kissed by an Angel, ... Tony Mowbray, Bookman, 1995

Lubo Moravcik: A Life Less Ordinary, ... Michael Zeman and Joe Sullivan, Celtic, 2001

Martin O'Neill: The Biography, ... Alex Montgomery, Virgin Books, 2003

Mo, ... Maurice Johnston, Mainstream, 1988

Odd Man Out, ... Brian McClair, Andre Deutsch, 1997

On Top With United, ... Pat Crerand and Ian Peebles, Stanley Paul, 1969

Over and Over: The Story of Seville, ... Anna Smith and Simon Houston, Daily Record, 2003

Paolo Di Canio, ... Paolo Di Canio (with Gabriele Marcotti), Collins Willow, 2000

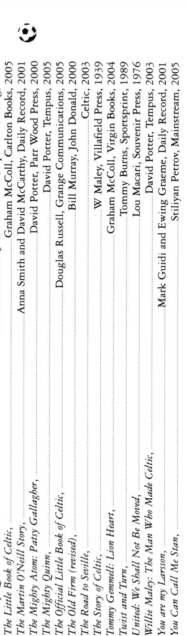

Paradise Lost, ... David Hay, Mainstream, 1988

Passed to You, ... Chalie Tully, Stanley Paul, 1958

Sure It's a Grand Old Team to Play For, ... Ronnie Simpson, Souvenir Press, 1967

Talking with Celtic, ... Eugene MacBride, Breedon Books, 2001

Ten Days That Shook Celtic, ... Tom Campbell, Fort, 2005

The Big Shot, ... Tommy Gemmell, Stanley Paul, 1968

The Essential History of Celtic, ... McColl and Sheridan, WH Smith, 2002

The Greatest Fans in the World, ... Celtic Supporters, UFB Publishers, 2004

The Head Bhoys, ... Graham McColl, Mainstream, 2002

The Hoops Quiz Book, ... John DT White, Apex Publishing, 2005

The Little Book of Celtic, ... Graham McColl, Carlton Books, 2005

The Martin O'Neill Story, ... Anna Smith and David McCarthy, Daily Record, 2001

The Mighty Atom: Patsy Gallagher, ... David Potter, Parr Wood Press, 2000

The Mighty Quinn, ... David Potter, Tempus, 2005

The Official Little Book of Celtic, ... Douglas Russell, Grange Communications, 2005

The Old Firm (revised), ... Bill Murray, John Donald, 2000

The Road to Seville, ... Celtic, 2003

The Story of Celtic, ... W Maley, Villafield Press, 1939

Tommy Gemmell: Lion Heart, ... Graham McColl, Virgin Books, 2004

Twist and Turn, ... Tommy Burns, Sportsprint, 1989

United: We Shall Not Be Moved, ... Lou Macari, Souvenir Press, 1976

Willie Maley: The Man Who Made Celtic, ... David Potter, Tempus, 2003

You are my Larsson, ... Mark Guidi and Ewing Graeme, Daily Record, 2001

You Can Call Me Stan, ... Stiliyan Petrov, Mainstream, 2005

🐝 CELTIC XI OF THE 1980s 🐝

Reserves
Allen *McKNIGHT* • Willie *McSTAY* • Billy *STARK*
Chris *MORRIS* • Frank *McAVENNIE*
Manager
David *HAY*

Did You Know That?
Jock Stein led Scotland to the 1982 World Cup finals only to see the Scots put out of the competition by the Soviet Union on goal difference.

🐝 THE BHOYS ARE BACK IN TOWN (17) 🐝

"This may sound blasé, but you get used to things like that. You don't even notice the size of the crowd really. I think you'd notice more if there was hardly anybody there."
Bobby Lennox, *on playing in front of 110,000 at the Bernabeu Stadium in Celtic's European Cup quarter-final second leg with Real Madrid in March 1980*

🐝 FOUR OUT OF FOUR 🐝

Season 2003–04 was the first time in the history of the Scottish Premier League, dating back to season 1975–76, that Celtic won all four league games against Rangers.

❧ CELTIC TRAIL BLUES BROTHERS ❧

Celtic sit in third place in the table for holding the record number of domestic Doubles behind Rangers and Northern Ireland's Linfield. Here is the all-time leader table:

Club	Nation	Number of Doubles
Linfield	Northern Ireland	17
Rangers	Scotland	17
Celtic	Scotland	13
HB	Faroe Islands	12
Muharraq	Bahrain	12
Al-Ahly	Egypt	11
Olympiakos	Greece	11
CSKA Sofia	Bulgaria	10
Dinamo Kiev	Ukraine	10
Levski Sofia	Bulgaria	10

❧ CELTIC HELP OUT A BLUE ❧

Celtic played Everton in Neville Southall's testimonial match.

❧ OLD FIRM'S CUP FINAL CONSISTENCY ❧

During the 20th century, the only year ending in "1" where one of the Old Firm teams were not represented in the Scottish Cup final was 1991 – no final was played in 1941 because of the Second World War.

1901	Hearts 4–3 Celtic
1911	Celtic 2–0 Hamilton Academicals (replay)
1921	Partick Thistle 1–0 Rangers
1931	Celtic 4–2 Motherwell (replay)
1941	Not staged
1951	Celtic 1–0 Motherwell
1961	Dunfermline 2–0 Celtic (replay)
1971	Celtic 2–1 Rangers (replay)
1981	Rangers 4–1 Dundee United (replay)
1991	Motherwell 4–3 Dundee United (aet)

❧ WEE GORDON LAST ❧

In 1991–92, Gordon Strachan was a member of the Leeds United side that won the last English First Division title before the Premiership.

✖✖ OUR BHOYS HAVE WON THE CUP (12) ✖✖

The 1988 Scottish Cup final was a remarkable game in which Celtic, celebrating their centenary season, won the Double. Dundee United took the lead just after half-time with a fine goal from Kevin Gallacher, but Celtic came back with two late goals from Frank McAvennie. A feature of this season had been Celtic's ability to score late goals when all seemed lost. It had happened in the semi-final against Hearts and now, once again, in the final. The other Dundee team had provided the opposition three weeks earlier when the league was won. It had been a wonderful campaign for the club's manager, Billy McNeill.

SCOTTISH FA CUP FINAL 1988
14 MAY 1988, HAMPDEN PARK, GLASGOW
Celtic (0) 2   **v**   **Dundee United** (0) 1
(McAvennie 2)   (Gallacher)
Att. 74,000
Celtic: McKnight, Morris, Rogan, Aitken, McCarthy, Whyte (Stark), Miller, McStay, McAvennie, Walker (McGhee), Burns.

✖✖ JOCK BROWN ✖✖

In June 1997, Jock Brown was appointed as the general manager of Glasgow Celtic Football Club. At the time of his appointment, Jock was a practising solicitor who specialized in sports law and he was a football commentator for BBC Scotland. Brown had never managed a football team prior to his appointment. Celtic's gamble did not pay off and Brown resigned his position on 7 November 1998.

Did You Know That?
In 1997, Celtic changed the football management set-up of the club. From the 1997–98 season until the arrival of Martin O'Neill in 2000, the club's head coach was required to deal with all matters relating to coaching, tactics and team selection. Meanwhile, the general manager's remit was to deal with contracts and general administration duties.

✖✖ THE McSTAY FAMILY TRADITION ✖✖

When Paul and his brother Willie McStay lifted the Scottish Cup with Celtic in 1985, they emulated the feat of their great-uncles, Willie and Jimmy McStay, in the 1920s.

❧ ALFIE CONN'S UNIQUE CUP DOUBLE ❧

Alfie Conn was the first player to win a Scottish FA Cup winners' medal with both Old Firm teams. He was in the Rangers team that beat Celtic 3–2 in the 1973 final and, in 1977, he helped Celtic beat Rangers 1–0 in the final.

❧ CELTIC ALMOST SUED ❧

One week prior to Celtic's 3–1 defeat to Rangers in the first-ever Old Firm Scottish Cup final on 17 February 1894[†] at Second Hampden Park, the grandstand at Celtic Park was severely damaged in a storm with debris being scattered all over the nearby Janefield cemetery. The newspaper stories at the time spoke of Celtic being sued for damages but nothing ever came of it.

❧ BEST OLD FIRM LEAGUE WIN IN 62 YEARS ❧

On 27 August 2000, Celtic beat Rangers 6–2 at Celtic Park in the Scottish Premier League. It was the Bhoys' best Old Firm league win since they hammered Rangers by the same score at Celtic Park on 10 September 1938.

❧ EXPLOSIVE START ❧

In the Scottish Premier League Old Firm game at Ibrox on 7 December 2002, Chris Sutton stunned the home fans with a goal after just 18 seconds. It was the fastest goal ever scored in an Old Firm game. However, Rangers recovered from this early shock and rallied to win 3–2.

❧ BIG JOCK MEETS JINKY ❧

Jock Stein was still the manager of Hibernian when Jimmy Johnstone was playing in a reserve match at Parkhead. By chance they met in the toilet and Big Jock expressed his surprise that Jimmy was playing in the reserves. "You're far too good a player for that," he told the little redhead, and Jimmy then realized that there was somebody who rated him.

[†]*Exactly one week after their 1894 Cup final defeat by Rangers, Celtic beat Rangers 3–2 at Celtic Park to clinch the Scottish First Division championship. After losing 5–0 to Rangers on 2 September 1893, Celtic went on a terrific run of 11 consecutive league victories.*

🎗 PAUL McSTAY 🎗

Paul McStay was born on 22 October 1964 in Hamilton and spent his entire career with Celtic. He was born of impeccable Celtic stock, with his great-uncles Willie and Jimmy McStay having already written many glorious pages in Celtic's history. Added to the latter, Paul's brother Willie was also destined for his share of Celtic glory.

Paul first came to Celtic's attention when he played at Wembley for the Scottish Schoolboys against their English counterparts in 1980. There was a tremendous amount of talent on the pitch that day, but Paul McStay outshone them all. In 1981, he signed for Celtic at just 17 years of age, when his father accompanied him to meet Billy McNeill, the Celtic manager, at Celtic Park. In January 1982, he made his debut in a Scottish Cup game at home to Queen of the South. He made a few more appearances that season and won the hearts of the Celtic faithful in the final game of the season in which Celtic were struggling to beat St Mirren. The score was 0–0 at half-time and the news from Pittodrie was that rivals Aberdeen were four ahead of Rangers who had mysteriously lost form. Had Celtic not beaten the Buddies, Aberdeen would have won the championship. However, a young McStay took charge of the midfield and Celtic ran out 3–0 winners to clinch the title.

It was the following season, 1982–83, that Scotland began to realize they had an outstanding player. Celtic won the League Cup and really should also have won the Scottish League championship and the Scottish Cup, but the football writers were impressed by the quality play of McStay. Many fans thought he possessed the silky playing skills of a Peter Wilson, the commitment of a Bobby Murdoch and the cannonball shot of a Neil Mochan.

The 1983–84 season was an unlucky one for Celtic, who were now under the temporary management of David Hay. However, Paul won the first of his 76 Scottish caps and scored for a heroic ten-man Celtic in the last minute of that desperately unlucky Scottish Cup final of 1984. Celtic made amends with victory in the following season's Cup final, and who can forget the last day of the 1985–86 season, when Paul was sensational as Celtic thrashed St Mirren 5–0 to win the league after Hearts buckled under the pressure at Dens Park.

Paul achieved the Double with Celtic in the centenary season of 1987–88 and was voted the Scottish PFA Player of the Year and the Scottish Football Writers' Association Player of the Year. In 1989, Paul lifted the Scottish Cup again with Celtic, was made club captain in 1990 and, in 1995, won his last trophy with Celtic, the Scottish Cup. Two years later, in April 1997, at Stark's Park, Kirkcaldy, Paul limped out of football to lead a much deserved quiet life.

🕸 CELTIC ON TOUR 🕸

1904

Vienna	Union Wien v Celtic	1–6	W
Vienna	Wiener AC v Celtic	2–4	W
Prague	SK Slavia Praha v Celtic	1–4	W

1906

Prague	SK Slavia Praha v Celtic	3–3	D
Leipzig	VfB Leipzig v Celtic	1–9	W

1907

Copenhagen	Boldklubben 1893 v Celtic	2–5	W
Copenhagen	Kobenhavn Select v Celtic	2–1	L
Copenhagen	Kobenhavn Select v Celtic	2–4	W

1911

Dresden	Select Dresden v Celtic	1–6	W
Prague	Deutscher FC Prag v Celtic	0–3	W
Prague	Deutscher FC Prag v Celtic	1–1	D
Budapest	Ferencvaros TC v Celtic	1–1	D
Vienna	Wiener Sport Club v Celtic	1–5	W
Vienna	Wiener Athletic Club v Celtic	1–2	W
Basle	FC Basle v Celtic	1–5	W
Paris	Red Star Paris v Celtic	1–8	W

🕸 A TEAM OF NUMBER SEVENS 🕸

In a fitting tribute to the legendary Jimmy Johnstone, who sadly passed away seven days earlier, Celtic lifted the CIS Cup after beating Dunfermline Athletic 3–0 in the final at Hampden Park on 19 March 2006. In memory of the little genius all of the Celtic players wore Jinky's No. 7 on their shorts to claim Gordon Strachan's first trophy for Celtic. The win also marked the first piece of silverware of Strachan's managerial career, which included stints at Coventry City and Southampton.

🕸 FIVE STRAIGHT "DOUBLES" 🕸

In 1970, Celtic won the Scottish League championship for the fifth consecutive year, and for the 25th time, as well as the Scottish League Cup for a fifth consecutive year, the seventh time they had won the competition.

✿ OUR BHOYS HAVE WON THE CUP (13) ✿

The 1995 Scottish Cup final was arguably one of the worst-ever finals to have been played, but it was very precious to Celtic supporters because it saw them claim their first trophy since 1989 and brought to an end a dreadful period in the club's history. Six months earlier, Celtic had lost to Raith Rovers in the League Cup final, and there were fears that this might happen again to Airdrie. But Pierre van Hooijdonk got an early goal and Celtic held onto their lead with the injured Peter Grant absolutely magnificent. Paul McStay collected the trophy, a fitting tribute to a loyal servant.

SCOTTISH FA CUP FINAL 1995
27 MAY 1995, HAMPDEN PARK, GLASGOW
Celtic (1) 1   v   **Airdrieonians (0) 0**
(van Hooijdonk)

Att. 36,915

Celtic: Bonner, Boyd, McKinlay, Vata, McNally,
Grant, McLaughlin, McStay, Van Hooijdonk (Falconer),
Donnelly (O'Donnell), Collins.

✿ THE BHOYS ARE BACK IN TOWN (18) ✿

"My only regret is that the team after the Lions never played long enough because we might have equalled what they had done in Europe. We were getting to semi-finals and we hadn't reached our peak."
David Hay *on Celtic's young players of the early 1970s*

✿ AN EXPENSIVE PROGRAMME ✿

The match programme published for the friendly match played between Everton and Celtic at Anfield on 5 April 1890 was sold in a sports memorabilia auction for £2,000. When Liverpool FC was formed in 1892, they took over Anfield and Everton moved to Goodison Park.

✿ "STAN THE MAN" ALMOST A BHOY ✿

On 30 September 2004, Stan Collymore released his autobiography, *Tackling My Demons*. In it he claimed that he had nearly signed for Celtic: "Martin [O'Neill] called my lawyer and said that he was planning a pairing of me and Chris Sutton in attack, with Henrik Larsson just behind us. It never happened."

❧ A JAGGY AFFAIR ❧

After suffering their first-ever loss to Partick Thistle in the 1892–93 season, Celtic had to visit Inchview once again for a Glasgow Cup tie later in the season. The Jags took the game so seriously that their committee set up special training for the game and gave a prize to the player who turned up most often for training. Unlike the case for their first encounter, Celtic paraded a strong side for this cup-tie. Thistle led 1–0 at half-time. Then Partick's Bruce had to leave the field for treatment and, before he returned, Celtic equalized and then scored a second goal late in the game.

At the following Glasgow FA meeting, Partick Thistle lodged a protest, claiming that Mulvey of Celtic had played a Lanarkshire Cup game for Carfin Shamrock, which made him ineligible for the Glasgow Cup tie. The protest was upheld and the game was replayed two weeks later. Celtic were furious with the decision and lodged a counter-protest concerning the gate transactions at Inchview. Following an investigation, a few members of Partick Thistle were found guilty of irregularities. However, Partick Thistle Football Club was absolved of any guilt, but ordered to correct the mistakes.

Upon arriving at Inchview for the replay, the Celtic board of directors were charged an admission fee to the pavilion. A crowd of 4,000, the highest ever at Inchview, saw Miller put the Jags into the lead after ten minutes. Thistle continued to have the better of the game, but Celtic equalized in the second half to take the game to a second replay at Celtic Park. Shortly after the game, rumours circulated that Celtic believed Campbell of Thistle to be an ineligible player. However, a Celtic official stated that Partick could have played 11 ineligible players and that Celtic would not have protested, instead electing to exact their revenge in the second replay.

At Celtic Park, the Partick Thistle committee were barred from the pavilion. The pressure certainly got to the Thistle players, as they scored two own goals during a crushing 8–0 defeat.

❧ LARSSON'S SHIRT SOLD AT AUCTION ❧

On 21 September 2004, ex-Celtic director Willie Haughey paid £3,346 for the kit worn by Henrik Larsson on his farewell appearance for Celtic at Celtic Park at a football memorabilia auction held by Christie's in London. Larsson wore the Celtic No. 7 shirt for a testimonial match against Seville.

❧ WILLIE MALEY ❧

William "Willie" Patrick Maley was born in Newry, Northern Ireland, on 25 April 1868, was the first manager of Celtic Football Club and was one of the most successful managers in the history of Scottish football. He managed Celtic for an astonishing 43 years, winning 30 major trophies during his time in charge. In 1888, he was signed by the newly formed Celtic Football Club and became one of the club's first players. In 1897, the board of directors at Celtic appointed Maley as their first secretary-manager. He was just 29 years old at the time but, in his first full season in charge, Celtic won the league championship. Maley's management style was of the "hands-off" variety: he never worked with his players in training, never participated in team talks and did not even talk to his players at either half-time or full-time. Indeed, he even watched the games from the directors' box. His players would only find out if they were playing in the next game by reading about it in the local newspaper.

When Maley took control of Celtic, they had been a buying club for the first ten years of their existence, spending heavily to bring professionals to Parkhead. Maley decided to place his faith in youth and relied almost entirely on recruiting young players fresh from junior football. He created a young team that won six league titles in a row between 1905 and 1910 and, under his leadership, Celtic won their first Double. In 1910, Celtic were genuinely considered to be the best team in world football, and the six-in-a-row record remained unbroken until the 1970s, when Jock Stein's heroes achieved nine-in-a-row. When Maley's six-in-a-row side grew old, he built a second great team that won four consecutive league titles between 1914 and 1917 and set what is still the United Kingdom record for an unbeaten run in professional football: 62 games (49 won, 13 drawn), from 13 November 1915 until 21 April 1917. His second great side won two further championships, in 1919 and 1922.

Celtic won more trophies during the 1920s and, in the mid-1930s, Maley built his third great team, featuring Jimmy Delaney and Jimmy McGrory. This team won the league championship in 1936 and 1938 and the Scottish Cup in 1937. By this time, Maley was approaching 70 years of age and his era at Celtic was about to end sourly. Celtic sat at the bottom of the league table and, following a meeting with the board of directors in February 1940, he was "retired". However, his place in the history of Glasgow Celtic Football Club is assured, as he helped turn Celtic into one of the most successful clubs in football.

🎗 CRERAND MAKES HIS SCOTLAND BOW 🎗

Following Scotland's 9–3 humiliation by England at Wembley on 15 April 1961, Scotland manager Ian McColl made six changes for their next game against the Republic of Ireland on 3 May 1961 in a World Cup qualifying game. Celtic's shell-shocked goalkeeper, Frank Haffey, was dropped; Billy McNeill was retained and won his second cap; while Paddy Crerand made his international debut. Scotland won 4–1.

🎗 DALGLISH MAKES SCOTLAND DEBUT 🎗

On 10 November 1971, Celtic's Kenny Dalglish made his international debut for Scotland in a 1–0 European Championship qualifying game win over Belgium at Pittodrie Stadium, Aberdeen. Dalglish came on as a second-half substitute for Alexander Cropley of Hibernian in the 48th minute of the game. Derby County's John O'Hare scored for Scotland.

🎗 MACARI AWESTRUCK BY BRAZILIANS 🎗

Celtic's Lou Macari played in the Scotland side that lost 1–0 to world champions Brazil on 5 July 1972 in the Brazil Independence Cup, in front of 130,000 fans at the Estadio do Maracana, Rio de Janeiro. Jairzinho scored for Brazil in a team that lined up as follows:

1	Leao
2	Ze Maria
3	Brito
4	Vantuir
5	Clodoaldo
6	Marco Antonio
7	Jairzihno
8	Gerson
9	Tostao
10	Leivinha *(sub. Dario)*
11	Rivelino

🎗 LUCKY COIN TOSS 🎗

When Celtic met Benfica in the second round of the 1969–70 European Cup, both legs ended as 3–0 home wins. The away goals rule did not exist then – nor would it have helped – so the referee tossed a coin to decide the winner. Luckily for Celtic, they made the right call.

❧ CELTIC XI OF THE 1990s ☙

Reserves
Pat *BONNER* • Rudi *VATA* • Alan *STUBBS*
Mark *RIEPER* • Darren *JACKSON*
Manager
Tommy *BURNS*

Did You Know That?

In 1996, Jorge Cadete's Scottish Football Association registration papers were deliberately delayed by Jim Farry, the then SFA chairman, at the same time that Celtic were going through a patchy period of form. Rangers went on to win the SPL and Scottish Cup double while Celtic lost only one SPL game all season. Farry was subsequently found guilty of misconduct and was sacked by the SFA, while Celtic received a mere £50,000 in compensation.

❧ LAMBERT'S OLD FIRM DEBUT ☙

On 7 November 1997, Paul Lambert[†] signed for Celtic from Borussia Dortmund. The following day he made his Celtic debut as a substitute in a 1–0 defeat at Rangers.

'Paul Lambert could have been a Rangers player two years before he joined Celtic. However, Rangers baulked at Motherwell's £1 million asking price. Lambert won a European Cup-winners' medal in 1997 with Borussia Dortmund.

❦ SAINT MUNGO CUP WINNERS ❧

In 1951, Celtic won the Saint Mungo Cup[†]. The cup was formed as part of the "Festival of Britain" celebrations. Saint Mungo is believed to have arrived in Glasgow around AD540. He built his church at the Molendinar Burn, where today's modern cathedral is situated. His ecclesiastical colleagues had given him the name "Mungo", meaning "Dear One". It is said that Saint Mungo performed four religious miracles in Glasgow, all of which are represented in the city's coat of arms. The following verse is sung to recall the miracles:

> *Here's the bird that never flew*
> *Here's the tree that never grew*
> *Here's the bell that never rang*
> *Here's the fish that never swam*

❦ KEANO MAKES HIS DEBUT ❧

Roy Keane[††] had a baptism of fire in his Celtic debut as they lost their Scottish Cup tie against Clyde, 2–1 at Broadwood Stadium.

❦ LISBON LIONS 2 NORTHERN IRELAND 1 ❧

No fewer than nine Old Firm players were in the Scotland side that beat Northern Ireland 2–1 at Hampden Park on 16 November 1966 in a Home International and European Championship group 8 game. Bobby Lennox scored on his international debut for Scotland with his Celtic Park team-mate, Bobby Murdoch, scoring Scotland's other goal.

❦ CRAIG MAKES HIS SCOTLAND DEBUT ❧

On 22 November 1967, Celtic's Jim Craig made his international debut for Scotland in a Home International and European Championship group game at Hampden Park. Scotland won 3–2 in front of a 57,472 crowd. Also in the Scotland team that day were Celtic's Jimmy Johnstone and Bobby Lennox.

[†]Glasgow's motto, "Let Glasgow flourish by the preaching of his word and the praising of his name," is a tribute to Saint Mungo. Saint Mungo's feast day is on 1 July. In 1993, the new St Mungo's Museum, the United Kingdom's only museum of religion, was officially opened.

[††]Keano was chosen for the "FIFA 100", a list of the 100 greatest living footballers, by the legendary Pele.

⚽ WE ARE THE CHAMPIONS (11) ⚽

Seldom has tension reigned so strongly in Glasgow as Rangers strove for ten championships in a row and Celtic managed to stop what would have been an irreversible blow to the club's fortunes. In the spring of 1998, first Celtic, then Rangers, threw games away, but it all came down to the last game of the season. Only a win against St Johnstone would guarantee Celtic the title. Henrik Larsson scored early, but it was only when Harald Brattbakk doubled their lead halfway through the second half that Celtic were crowned champions. The green half of Glasgow celebrated, but the green half of Edinburgh mourned as Hibernian went down.

Scottish League 1997–98
Premier Division

	P		Home					Away				Pts
		W	D	L	F	A	W	D	L	F	A	
1. Celtic	36	12	4	2	41	9	10	4	4	23	15	74
2. Rangers	36	13	4	1	46	16	8	5	5	30	22	72
3. Heart of Midlothian	36	10	5	3	36	24	9	5	4	34	22	67
4. Kilmarnock	36	9	4	5	24	21	4	7	7	16	31	50
5. St Johnstone	36	7	5	6	20	21	6	4	8	18	21	48
6. Aberdeen	36	6	6	6	20	18	3	6	9	19	35	39
7. Dundee United	36	5	7	6	23	18	3	6	9	20	33	37
8. Dunfermline Athletic	36	4	9	5	26	30	4	4	10	17	38	36
9. Motherwell	36	6	4	8	26	28	3	3	12	20	36	34
10. Hibernian	36	6	4	8	26	24	0	8	10	12	35	30

Dundee promoted.

⚽ THE BHOYS ARE BACK IN TOWN (19) ⚽

"If someone says to me, 'What about that goal you scored in the European Cup final?' invariably they are talking about Lisbon and 1967. No one ever mentions the goal I scored against Feyenoord. It just shows you: when you are losers no one wants to know. When you are winners, everybody wants to know."
Tommy Gemmell, *1995*

⚽ FOUR FROM SIX ⚽

In 2005–06, Celtic won their fourth SPL championship in six years.

❧ WIM JANSEN ☙

At the beginning of July 1997, Wim Jansen was appointed as Celtic's head coach and was handed the seemingly daunting task of preventing Rangers from winning their tenth consecutive league title. Jansen had played for Feyenoord from 1966 to 1980, making 474 appearances and scoring 41 goals for the Dutch side. He had played in the European Cup final win over Celtic in 1970 and had also been in the Feyenoord side that defeated Tottenham Hotspur in the 1974 UEFA Cup final. In 1970, he won the World Club Championship with the Dutch champions and ended his playing career with brief spells with the Washington Diplomats and Ajax. Wim won 65 caps for Holland and played in both the 1974 and 1978 World Cup finals. Prior to taking control of Celtic, Wim had coached the Feyenoord youth team, Lokeren of Belgium, SVV Dorrecht and Feyenoord in Holland and Sanfrecce Hiroshima in Japan. The Dutchman was an instant success at Celtic Park, leading the team to victory in the 1997 Coca-Cola Cup final, and he will forever hold a special place in the hearts of all Celtic fans because of the fact that he brought the Scottish Premier League title to Celtic at the end of his first season in charge. Unbelievably, Wim resigned on 11 May 1998.

❧ CELEBRITY CELTS ☙

Alan McManus *(snooker)*
Ardal O'Hanlon
Billy Connolly
Bono *(U2)*
Claire Grogan *(Altered Images)*
Dominik Diamond
Elaine C. Smith
Fran Healy
Jim Kerr *(Simple Minds)*
John Higgins *(snooker)*
Martine McCutcheon

Michael Caton Jones
Mogwai *(band)*
Primal Scream
Rod Stewart
Ruaraidh Fitzpatrick
Shane McGowan *(The Pogues)*
Sharleen Spiteri *(Texas)*
Steve Collins *(boxer)*
Teenage Fanclub
Tony Roper
Liam Gallagher *(Oasis)*

❧ 30 YEARS ON, SAME RESULT ☙

Thirty years after losing their first-ever European tie in a penalty shoot-out, Celtic suffered the same fate again when Valencia put them out of the 2001–02 UEFA Cup after a penalty shoot-out. Celtic lost the away leg 0–1 and won the home leg 1–0, but went out of the competition 5–4 on penalties.

❧ BOBBY MURDOCH ❧

Bobby Murdoch made his debut on the opening day of the 1962–63 season, scoring against Hearts in the League Cup, but any early promise fizzled out as he was tried out all over the dysfunctional forward line of that time. In the 1963 Scottish Cup final, Bobby scored the equalizer against Rangers, but the forward line was then re-jigged for the replay with Jimmy Johnstone and Frank Brogan dropped.

Impatient and frustrated fans often turned on Bobby during Celtic's trophyless years of 1963 and 1964. By Christmas 1964, Bobby contemplated emigrating to Australia with his young family, but just like Billy McNeill, things started to improve for Murdoch when Jock Stein arrived to take charge of Celtic at the end of January 1965. Big Jock quickly realized that Murdoch's prodigious talent was somewhat misplaced in the forward line and, after a few games, moved him to his natural habitat of right-half. The effect was instantaneous and dramatic and turned out to be Stein's greatest ever masterstroke. A trophy followed a few months later, following the Scottish Cup final win over Dunfermline Athletic.

Murdoch was the complete player: a superb passer, an aggressive ball-winner, a tenacious tackler in defence when required and a player capable of scoring a few goals. He teamed up with Jimmy Johnstone on the right and Bertie Auld in midfield and it wasn't long before the very same fans that once doubted his ability were comparing him with Celtic legends Sunny Jim and Peter Wilson. In the late 1960s, all of Europe reluctantly but genuinely agreed that Celtic played the best football of the day and that Bobby Murdoch was the greatest midfield player of that decade.

Bobby was not so fortunate on the international scene, however. He played against England at Hampden in 1966 when not feeling well and again in 1969, when the entire Scotland team played poorly in a 4–1 defeat at Wembley. However, he did score a great goal against West Germany in a World Cup qualifier in 1969.

Bobby was plagued with a recurring ankle injury, which he first picked up in 1964, and he also suffered from a weight problem, which he and Stein had to work at with visits to health farms and intensive training. In 1973, following nearly a decade of consistent success at Celtic, Bobby moved to Middlesbrough to team up with Jackie Charlton, where he helped the Teessiders win the Second Division championship in his first season at the club. In 1976, his ankle became so bad that he could not continue playing, but he remained at Boro as a coach and eventually as manager. Bobby died in May 2001 after a long period of ill health.

❧ KENNAWAY WINS FIRST CAP ❧

Celtic's goalkeeper, Joe Kennaway, won his first international cap for Scotland in the team that drew 2–2 with Austria at Hampden Park on 29 November 1933. It was the first time that a continental team had played an international in Scotland.

❧ CELTIC 0 RUSSIA 2 ❧

Seven Celtic players played in Scotland's 2–0 defeat by Russia on 10 May 1967 in an international friendly match at Hampden Park in front of 53,497 fans. The seven Celtic players were: Ronald Campbell, Tommy Gemmell[†], John Clark, Billy McNeill, Jimmy Johnstone, Bobby Lennox and Willie Wallace, who came on as a substitute for Denis Law.

❧ HUGHES NETS AGAINST WORLD CHAMPS ❧

Celtic's John Hughes scored on his sixth appearance for Scotland against world champions England in a 1–1 draw at Hampden Park on 24 February 1968 in a Home International and European Championship group game in front of a crowd of 134,000. His club team-mates Ronnie Simpson, Tommy Gemmell, Billy McNeill and Bobby Lennox also played.

❧ DANISH DELIGHT FOR LENNOX ❧

On 16 October 1968, Celtic's Bobby Lennox, winning his sixth cap, scored the only goal of the game in the 70th minute to give Scotland a 1–0 win over Denmark in an international friendly at Idraetsparken, Copenhagen.

❧ NOT SO CZECH MATE ❧

Celtic's Paddy Crerand[††] and Czechoslovakia's Andrej Kvasnak were sent off in the 35th minute for fighting during Scotland's 4–0 defeat by Czechoslovakia on 14 May 1961 in a World Cup qualifying group game. The game was played in front of a partisan crowd of 48,000 fans in the Tehelne Pole Stadion, Bratislava.

[†] *Tommy Gemmell scored an own goal in the 17th minute of the game.*
[††] *It was only the third time that Crerand had played for his country, while Kvasnak had slotted home a penalty 23 minutes before he was dismissed.*

✿❧ EUROPEAN NIGHT OF PRIDE ❧✿

Although Celtic lost the 2003 UEFA Cup final to Porto of Portugal, it turned out to be a glorious victory for all connected with the club as 80,000 fans showed everything that was good about Celtic and Scotland by going to Seville, having a great time and winning awards. Henrik Larsson scored twice for Celtic, but it was not enough on the night. En route, Celtic had defeated Blackburn Rovers and Liverpool, two victories which made some of the English media swallow a few words they had previously written about Martin O'Neill's team.

UEFA CUP FINAL 2003
21 MAY 2003, ESTADIO OLIMPICO, SEVILLE

Porto (1) 3   v   **Celtic** (0) 2
(Derlei 45, 115,   (Larsson 47, 57)
Alenichev 54)

After extra time; Porto won on golden goal
Att. 52,972

Celtic: Douglas, Mjallby, Balde, Valgaeren (Laursen), Agathe, Lambert (McNamara), Lennon, Petrov, Thompson; Larsson, Sutton.

Porto: Baia, P. Ferreira, J. Costa (Emanuel), Valente, Carvalho, Maniche, Costinha (R. Costa), Deco, Alenichev, Derlei; Capucho (M. Ferreira).

✿❧ TWO FROM TWO FOR MURDOCH ❧✿

On 16 April 1969, Celtic's Bobby Murdoch scored in his second consecutive international for Scotland in their 1–1 draw with West Germany in a World Cup qualifying group game at Hampden Park. Although Scotland failed to make it to the following year's World Cup finals in Mexico, West Germany did. They lost in the semi-finals, after having beaten England in the quarter-finals in Leon.

✿❧ JINKY SCORES AGAINST WEST GERMANY ❧✿

Celtic's Jimmy Johnstone scored in Scotland's 3–2 defeat by West Germany on 22 October 1969 in a World Cup qualifying group game in the Volksparkstadion, Hamburg.

✿❧ BIRTHDAY BOY ❧✿

John Hartson scored the goal that won the 2005–06 Scottish Premier League championship for Celtic on his 31st birthday.

❧ HAY, ONE IN FOUR ☙

Celtic's David Hay made his international debut for Scotland on 18 April 1970 in a Home International match against Northern Ireland at Windsor Park, Belfast. Scotland won 1–0, thanks to a goal from John O'Hare (Derby County), who was making his debut alongside Hay, Willie Carr (Coventry City) and Willie Dickson (Kilmarnock).

❧ ENGLAND'S UNBEATEN STREAK ENDED ☙

England's longest unbeaten streak stands at 20 matches played between the 3–2 home defeat to Scotland on 13 April 1889 and the 2–1 away defeat to Scotland at Celtic Park on 4 April 1896. England's record during this seven-year streak was 16 wins and four defeats (nine of the 20 matches were played at home). Celtic's James Blessington was in the Scotland team that brought England's record unbeaten streak to an end[†].

❧ SCOTLAND'S RECORD WIN ☙

On 23 February 1901, Scotland beat Ireland 11–0 in the Home International championships at Celtic Park in front of 15,000 fans. The 11–0 win is Scotland's record victory of all time and 7 of the goals were scored by Celtic players: Alexander McMahon (4), John Campbell (2) and David Russell (1). The remaining four goals were scored by Robert Hamilton (Rangers).

❧ HISTORIC GAME FOR SCOTLAND ☙

On 18 May 1930, Scotland played their first official international match abroad, beating France 2–0 in the Stade de Colombes, Paris. Celtic's John Thomson made his international debut in goal for the Scots, while his Celtic team-mate, Peter Wilson, was playing in only his second international. Hughie Gallacher of Newcastle United scored both goals.

❧ TWENTY MEDALS IN NINE YEARS ☙

Bobby Murdoch won nine Scottish titles in a row, the European Cup, five Scottish Cups and five Scottish League Cups with Celtic between 1965 and 1973.

[†] *Before 1900, England only played three times per year, once each against the other home countries, Scotland, Ireland and Wales in the Home International championship.*

❧ CELTIC XI OF THE 21st CENTURY ☙

1
Artur
BORUC

2
Jackie
McNAMARA

4
Bobo
BALDE

5
Johan
MJALLBY

3
Mark
WILSON

6
Roy
KEAN

7
Shaun
MALONEY

8
Stilian
PETROV

10
Chris
SUTTON

9
Henrik
LARSSON

11
Maciej
ZURAWSKI

Reserves
David *MARSHALL* • Neil *LENNON* • Joos *VALGAEREN*
Paul *LAMBERT* • John *HARTSON*
Manager
Gordon *STRACHAN*

Did You Know That?
Celtic hold the SPL record for an unbeaten run of home matches
(77) which was achieved between 2001 and 2004, and also hold
the record for the longest run of consecutive wins in a single season
(25 matches).

❧ THE BHOYS ARE BACK IN TOWN (20) ☙

"I'm often asked how this Rangers team compares with the Lisbon
Lions. I have to be honest and say I think it would be a draw but,
then, some of us are getting on for 60."
Bertie Auld, *in 1993, after Rangers had reached the group stage of the*
Champions League for the first time

❧ 40 UP ☙

When Celtic won the Scottish Premier League championship in
2005–06, it was their 40th league title.

❧ THE TREBLE MASTERS ☙

Celtic have won the Treble, consisting of the Scottish League championship, the Scottish FA Cup and the Scottish League Cup, three times: in 1967, 1969 and 2001.

❧ BIG JOCK SAVES DUNFERMLINE ☙

Jock Stein took up his first job as manager in the 1959–60 season, when he joined Dunfermline Athletic. Under Jock's astute leadership, Dunfermline won their last six league games to avoid relegation to the Second Division. During the season, Dunfermline lost 4–2 to Celtic at Celtic Park, but they won the return fixture 3–2.

❧ FOUNDER MEMBERS ☙

Of the 11 clubs that formed the original Scottish League in 1891–92, only Celtic and five others are still league teams (Clyde, Dumbarton, Hearts, Rangers and St Mirren).

❧ McGRORY'S FIVE-IN-A-ROW ☙

Celtic's Jimmy McGrory scored in five consecutive games for Scotland between 28 March 1931 and 1 April 1933 – versus England (h), Northern Ireland (h), Wales (a), Northern Ireland (a) and England (h).

❧ McGRAIN'S DOUBLE 16 ☙

Celtic's Danny McGrain won 62 caps for Scotland during his career with 32 of them coming in two 16-game consecutive runs.

❧ FANCY DRESS COSTUMES ☙

The 1890–91 season began in a very light-hearted way, with a charity fancy dress match at Partick Thistle's Inchview ground. The Irving Dramatic Club took on Minerva, with Celtic stars Willie Groves and Willie Maley taking part.

❧ STRACHAN'S CUP DOUBLE ☙

Apart from Martin Buchan, Gordon Strachan is the only player to have won a Scottish Cup winners' medal with Aberdeen and an English FA Cup winners' medal with Manchester United.

❧ OVER AND OVER ☙

Oh! over and over, we will follow you,
Over and over, we will see you through,
We're Celtic supporters, faithful through and through,
And over and over, we will follow you.
If you go to Germany, you will see us there,
France or Spain it's all the same,
We'll go anywhere,
We'll be there to cheer you,
As you travel round,
You can take us anywhere, we won't let you down.
Oh! over and over, we will follow you,
Over and over, we will see you through,
We're Celtic supporters, faithful through and through,
And over and over, we will follow you.
If you go to Lisbon, we'll go once again,
In Zaire you'll find us there calling out your name,
When you need supporting, you will always know,
We'll be right there with you, everywhere you go.
Oh! over and over, we will follow you,
Over and over, we will see you through,
We're Celtic supporters, faithful through and through,
And over and over, we will follow you.

❧ CELTIC'S FIRST CUP FINAL GOAL ☙

Celtic's first goal in the Scottish Cup final was scored by McCallum in their 1–2 defeat at the hands of Third Lanark on 9 February 1889.

❧ FOUR-IN-A-ROW FOR SCOTLAND ☙

Celtic's John Collins scored in four consecutive European Championship qualifying games for Scotland between 27 March 1991 and 12 October 1994 – versus Bulgaria (h), Romania (h), Finland (a) and the Faroe Islands (h).

❧ BLACK DAY FOR CELTIC ☙

On 12 February 1983, Eric Black of Aberdeen was the last player to score a hat-trick against Celtic. Forty thousand fans at Parkhead watched on as Aberdeen's victory leap-frogged them above Celtic to the top of the league.

❦ MARTIN O'NEILL ❧

In July 2000, Martin O'Neill arrived at Celtic Park like a breath of fresh air. Following a successful spell as manager of Leicester City, the Irishman set about turning an ailing team into one of winners. O'Neill quickly realized that he needed a rock upon which he could build his team, so he signed defenders Jood Valgaeren and Bobo Balde to help tighten up what had become a leaky defence. He then purchased Chris Sutton and John Hartson to help out Henrik Larsson in attack. O'Neill's management style paid off big time when, at the end of his first season in charge, Celtic collected the Treble. They successfully defended their SPL title the following season.

However, the one thing that O'Neill did for Celtic – something that no other manger since the halcyon days of Jock Stein had done before him – was to turn Celtic into a European force once again. Although Celtic had limited success in the Champions League, O'Neill's team made it all the way to the UEFA Cup final in 2003. An estimated 80,000 Celtic fans followed the team to Seville, Spain, only to see their team fall to a heartbreaking 3–2 defeat in extra time to Jose Mourinho's Porto. However, regardless of how difficult a pill the defeat must have been to swallow, at least the Celtic fans could assure themselves that the club's pride in Europe had been restored both on and off the pitch. In May 2005, Martin O'Neill left the club to care for his wife who was very ill and just missed out on securing a fourth SPL title. During his five years in charge, Martin O'Neill won three SPL championships, three Scottish Cups and one League Cup and there is no doubt that his place in the hearts of all Celtic fans is secure.

Did You Know That?
Martin O'Neill won 62 international caps for Northern Ireland and captained the side during the 1982 World Cup finals in Spain.

❦ CELTIC OUTCLASS THE WEE ROVERS ❧

Celtic first met Albion Rovers, nicknamed "The Wee Rovers", in the Scottish First Division in the 1919–20 season, winning 3–0 at Celtic Park and 5–0 at Cliftonhill.

❦ CELTIC 9 VALE OF LEVEN 1 ❧

In the 1890–91 season, Celtic beat Vale of Leven 9–1 in the Scottish First Division to record their biggest-ever win over them.

🏴 CELTIC'S RECORD UNBEATEN RUN 🏴

The following list details Celtic's remarkable 62-match unbeaten run between 20 November 1915 and 14 April 1917.

1915–16

Match	Date	Opponent		Score
	13/11/15	Heart of Midlothian	(a)	0–2 (lost)
1	20/11/15	Kilmarnock	(h)	2–0
2	27/11/15	Raith Rovers	(a)	2–0
3	4/12/15	Queen's Park	(h)	6–2
4	11/12/15	Ayr United	(a)	4–0
5	18/12/15	Partick Thistle	(a)	4–0
6	25/12/15	Airdrieonians	(h)	6–0
7	1/1/16	Rangers	(h)	2–2
8	3/1/16	Clyde	(a)	3–1
9	8/1/16	Dumbarton	(a)	2–1
10	15/1/16	Hibernian	(h)	3–1
11	22/1/16	Third Lanark	(a)	4–0
12	29/1/16	Ayr United	(h)	3–1
13	5/2/16	Aberdeen	(a)	4–0
14	12/2/16	Dumbarton	(h)	6–0
15	19/2/16	Queen's Park	(a)	1–0
16	26/2/16	Dundee	(h)	3–0
17	4/3/16	Kilmarnock	(a)	3–0
18	11/3/16	Hamilton Academicals	(h)	5–1
19	18/3/16	St Mirren	(a)	5–0
20	1/4/16	Morton	(h)	0–0
21	8/4/16	Falkirk	(a)	2–0
22	15/4/16	Raith Rovers	(h)	6–0
23	15/4/16	Motherwell	(a)	3–1
24	22/4/16	Heart of Midlothian	(h)	0–0
25	24/4/16	Third Lanark	(h)	4–1
26	29/4/16	Partick Thistle	(h)	5–0

1916–17

Match	Date	Opponent		Score
27	19/8/16	St Mirren	(a)	5–1
28	26/8/16	Hibernian	(h)	3–1
29	2/9/16	Ayr United	(a)	1–0
30	9/9/16	Airdrieonians	(h)	3–1
31	16/9/16	Motherwell	(a)	4–0

32	30/9/16	Heart of Midlothian	(h)	1–0
33	14/10/16	Falkirk	(a)	1–1
34	21/10/16	Morton	(h)	0–0
35	28/10/16	Rangers	(h)	0–0
36	4/11/16	Dundee	(a)	2–1
37	11/11/16	Queen's Park	(a)	3–1
38	18/11/16	Partick Thistle	(h)	0–0
39	25/11/16	Aberdeen	(h)	1–0
40	2/12/16	Raith Rovers	(a)	4–1
41	9/12/16	Ayr United	(h)	5–0
42	16/12/16	Hamilton Academicals	(a)	4–0
43	23/12/16	Partick Thistle	(a)	2–0
44	30/12/16	Falkirk	(h)	2–0
45	1/1/17	Rangers	(a)	0–0
46	2/1/17	Clyde	(h)	0–0
47	6/1/17	Motherwell	(h)	1–0
48	13/1/17	Heart of Midlothian	(a)	1–0
49	20/1/17	Dumbarton	(h)	1–1
50	27/1/17	Third Lanark	(a)	0–0
51	3/2/17	Raith Rovers	(h)	5–0
52	10/2/17	Morton	(a)	1–0
53	17/2/17	Dundee	(h)	2–0
54	24/2/17	Kilmarnock	(a)	2–2
55	3/3/17	Queen's Park	(h)	3–2
56	10/3/17	Hamilton Academicals	(h)	6–1
57	17/3/17	Airdrieonians	(a)	2–1
58	24/3/17	Aberdeen	(a)	0–0
59	31/3/17	St Mirren	(h)	3–0
60	7/4/17	Dumbarton	(a)	3–1
61	9/4/17	Third Lanark	(h)	2–0
62	14/4/17	Hibernian	(a)	1–0
	21/4/17	Kilmarnock	(h)	0–2 (lost)

Celtic's total record during this period was:

P	W	D	L	F	A	Pts
62	49	13	0	162	26	111

Did You Know That?

Two players, left-back Joseph Dodds and goalkeeper Charles Shaw, appeared in all 62 matches. The most common result in the run was a 0–0 draw, which occurred nine times. Celtic achieved 1–0 and 3–1 victories eight times each and a 2–0 win seven times.

❧ JOCK STEIN ☙

In a recent poll, Jock Stein was voted the greatest Scottish manager ever. In his 13 years as manager of Celtic, he won 25 domestic trophies and the European Cup. Stein, a former Celtic player, had his own playing career ended prematurely as a result of a bad ankle injury, but performed a pivotal role at Celtic during the 1950s as a coach and scout. In 1960, the lure of a management role at Dunfermline Athletic was too tempting for Stein to turn down and so he packed his kit bag and headed for East End Park. The Pars were faced with the threat of relegation to the Scottish Second Division when the Big Man arrived, but he transformed the club within six weeks, saving them from relegation and guiding them to the Scottish Cup final, where they defeated Celtic. From Dunfermline the Big Man moved on to Hibernian where he did not enjoy the same success but, in 1965, he took charge at Celtic Park.

Celtic dominated Scottish football under Stein's astute leadership for the next 13 years, winning ten Scottish League titles (including the famous nine-in-a-row), seven Scottish Cups, six League Cups and, of course, the European Cup. Perhaps the biggest disappointment for Celtic during Stein's reign – and even that was a remarkable achievement – was their 1970 European Cup final defeat to the Dutch champions Feyenoord. In July 1975, Jock almost lost his life in a horrific car crash and was away from the game for a year. He returned 12 months later, guiding Celtic to the Double of Scottish Cup and the first-ever Scottish Premier League title in 1977, his tenth and last as manager.

Prior to the beginning of the 1977–78 season, Stein's talisman, Kenny Dalglish, had left for Liverpool, while injuries to both Conn and Stanton ended any dreams of the European Cup returning to Paradise. Stein left Celtic amid rumours of a bust-up with the Celtic board and, after a brief spell managing Leeds United, he was appointed Scotland manager.

On 10 September 1985, the football world went into collective mourning following the tragic news that Jock Stein had died. That night Scotland were playing a World Cup qualifying game against Wales, at the Arms Park in Cardiff. The Scots needed just a draw to qualify for the 1986 World Cup finals in Mexico as runners-up behind group winners Spain. Wales took the lead, but when Scotland scored a late equalizer to end the game 1–1, Stein suffered a heart attack, from which he later died.

He will live forever in the heart of every Celtic fan and will always be fondly remembered as "The Lion King".

Did You Know That?

A journalist once described the Great Man as "a Protestant chieftain emerging from a Catholic stronghold to win great battles and memorable glories for the grand old club", and regaining for Celtic supporters "a paradise they must have once thought lost forever". No wonder then that the Celtic faithful refer to Celtic Park as "Paradise".

🎉 WE ARE THE CHAMPIONS (12) 🎉

Following a draw at Dunfermline on the first day of the 2003–04 season, Celtic went on an incredible run that saw them remain undefeated until the title had been won. Celtic also collected the Scottish Cup that year, but disappointments came their way both in Europe and in the League Cup, which was eventually won by Livingston, who were managed by former Celtic legend, David Hay.

Scottish League 2003–04
Premier Division

		Home					Away					
	P	W	D	L	F	A	W	D	L	F	A	Pts
1. Celtic	38	15	2	2	62	15	16	3	0	43	10	98
2. Rangers	38	16	0	3	48	11	9	6	4	28	22	81
3. Heart of Midlothian	38	12	5	2	32	17	7	6	6	24	23	68
4. Dunfermline Athletic	38	9	7	3	28	19	5	4	10	17	33	53
5. Dundee United	38	8	6	5	28	27	5	4	10	19	33	49
6. Motherwell	38	7	7	5	25	22	5	3	11	17	27	46
7. Dundee	38	8	3	8	21	20	4	7	8	27	37	46
8. Hibernian	38	6	5	8	25	28	5	6	8	16	32	44
9. Livingston	38	6	9	4	24	18	4	4	11	24	39	43
10. Kilmarnock	38	8	3	8	29	31	4	3	12	22	43	42
11. Aberdeen	38	5	3	11	22	29	4	4	11	17	34	34
12. Partick Thistle	38	5	4	10	24	32	1	4	14	15	35	26

Inverness Caledonian Thistle promoted.

🎉 BACK TO THE FUTURE 🎉

Two future Celtic players were on the scoresheet in the 1990–91 English FA Cup final. Ian Wright of Crystal Palace – who signed for the Bhoys in October 1999 – grabbed two goals in a 3–3 draw with Manchester United. United's Lee Martin, who would join in January 1994, scored the only goal of the replay.

❦ OUR BHOYS HAVE WON THE CUP (14) ❦

Celtic did remarkably well to come back in this Scottish Cup final only six days after Black Sunday, on which the Scottish League championship had been thrown away at Motherwell. In addition, there was the news that Martin O'Neill was leaving the club to look after his sick wife. How appropriate it was then that Martin O'Neill should be presented with the Scottish Cup that day.

SCOTTISH FA CUP FINAL 2005
28 MAY 2005, HAMPDEN PARK, GLASGOW
Celtic (1) 1   v   **Dundee United** (0) 0
(Thompson 11)
Att. 50,635
Celtic: Douglas, Agathe, Balde, Varga, McNamara, Petrov, Lennon, Sutton, Thompson (McGeady), Hartson (Valgaeren), Bellamy.

❦ WE ARE THE CHAMPIONS (13) ❦

Celtic's 2005–06 SPL Championship win was a triumph of consistency, determination and perserverance, and it showed the emergence of talented young players in Shaun Maloney, Steve McManus and Mark Wilson. The arrival of Gordon Strachan and the signing of Roy Keane had psychological benefits to the team on and off the pitch.

Scottish League 2005–06
Premier Division

		P		Home					Away				Pts
		P	W	D	L	F	A	W	D	L	F	A	Pts
1	Celtic	38	14	4	1	41	15	14	3	2	52	22	91
2	Heart of Midlothian	38	15	2	2	43	9	7	6	6	28	22	74
3	Rangers	38	13	4	2	38	11	8	6	5	29	26	73
4	Hibernian	38	11	1	7	39	24	6	4	9	22	32	56
5	Kilmarnock	38	11	3	5	39	29	4	7	8	24	35	55
6	Aberdeen	38	8	9	3	30	17	5	6	7	16	23	54
7	Inverness CT	38	5	6	7	21	21	10	7	3	30	17	58
8	Motherwell	38	7	5	7	35	31	6	5	8	20	30	49
9	Dundee Utd	38	5	8	6	22	28	2	4	13	19	38	33
10	Falkirk	38	2	6	11	14	30	6	3	10	21	34	33
11.	Dunfermline	38	3	5	11	17	39	5	4	10	16	29	33
12	Partick Thistle	38	5	4	10	24	32	1	4	14	15	35	26

❧ JOZEF VENGLOS ☙

Two months after the shock resignation of Wim Jansen, Jozef Venglos was appointed as head coach of Celtic on 17 July 1998. Venglos came to Celtic with an impressive résumé as both a player and a coach. Venglos was a Czechoslovakian international midfielder. As a coach he won the Czechoslovakian championship with Slovan Bratislava twice as well as being runner-up in the European Cup-Winners' Cup. He also coached Sporting Lisbon (1983–84), Aston Villa (1990–91) and Fenerbahce (1991–93), in addition to the national teams of Australia, Malaysia, Oman, Slovakia and Czechoslovakia. His greatest achievement in football came in 1976, when he led Czechoslovakia to victory in the European Championship finals, beating Holland in the semi-finals and West Germany in the final.

As well as his on-field achievements, he was also a coaching advisor to FIFA, the technical director to Slovan Bratislava and he possessed a doctorate in physical education as well as specializing in psychology. He speaks four languages and has co-ordinated FIFA study groups at the World Cup in Mexico in 1986, USA in 1994 and France in 1998.

However, he only spent one season in charge at Celtic Park and it ended without any silverware. At the end of the 1998–99, season Venglos took up a new position of European technical advisor, but remained at Celtic to help out the incoming manager, John Barnes.

Did You Know That?
In 1995, Jozef Venglos was appointed president of the European Coaches' Union and was chosen to coach the European and World Select XIs during the 1980s and 1990s.

❧ GORDON STRACHAN ☙

Gordon Strachan began his professional career at Dundee before joining Aberdeen. Part of Alex Ferguson's all-conquering side, Strachan won two Scottish League Championships, three Scottish Cups, the European Cup Winners' Cup and the European Super Cup. In 1984, he signed for Manchester United and won the FA Cup with the Red Devils in 1986. He left Old Trafford in 1989 and signed for Leeds United, where he helped the team to the First Division Championship in 1991–92. In 1995, he joined Coventry City as a player-coach and went on to manage them, and Southampton, before taking charge of Celtic in 2005.

🏴 CELTIC MANAGERS XI 🏴

1
Ronnie
SIMPSON
(Hamilton Academical)

2
David
HAY
(Motherwell)

4
Tommy
BURNS
(Kilmarnock)

5
Bertie
AULD
(Partick Thistle)

3
Billy
McNEILL
(Manchester City)

6
Roy
AITKEN
(Aston Villa)

7
Kenny
DALGLISH
(Liverpool)

8
Lou
MACARI
(West Ham)

10
Jimmy
McGRORY
(Kilmarnock)

9
John "Yogi"
HUGHES
(Stranraer)

11
Paul
LAMBERT
(Livingston)

Reserves
Murdo *MacLEOD* (Dumbarton) • Willie *MALEY* (Celtic) • Tony *MOWBRAY* (Hibernian)
Mo *JOHNSTON* (MetroStars) • John *HUGHES* (Falkirk)
Manager
Mick *McCARTHY* (Republic of Ireland)

Did You Know That?

When Mick McCarthy was the Republic of Ireland manager he sent Roy Keane home from Ireland's World Cup training camp in Saipan a few days before their 2002 World Cup campaign began. The McCarthy-Keane spat was later re-enacted on the stage in the hit play *I Keano*.

🏴 THE BHOYS ARE BACK IN TOWN (21) 🏴

"For a while I did unite Rangers and Celtic fans. There were people in both camps who hated me."
Mo Johnston, who played for both Old Firm sides

🏴 NEVER RELEGATED 🏴

Four clubs, Aberdeen, Celtic, Inverness Caley Thistle and Rangers, have never been relegated from the top division in Scottish football. The Glasgow giants' record stretches back to 1890, Aberdeen's to 1905, but Inverness did not reach this level until 2004.

🏵 FOR THE RECORD 🏵

Scottish League
1890–91 to 1925–26

		Home					Away					
	P	W	D	L	F	A	W	D	L	F	A	Pts	Pos
1890–91	18	7	2	0	26	8	4	1	4	22	13	21	3rd
1891–92	22	10	1	0	32	6	6	2	3	30	15	35	2nd
1892–93	18	8	0	1	32	14	6	1	2	22	11	29	1st
1893–94	18	7	1	1	30	12	7	0	2	23	20	29	1st
1894–95	18	6	2	1	30	14	5	2	2	20	15	26	2nd
1895–96	18	8	0	1	39	9	7	0	2	25	16	30	1st
1896–97	18	6	2	1	20	5	4	2	3	22	13	24	4th
1897–98	18	8	1	0	30	7	7	2	0	26	6	33	1st
1898–99	18	7	0	2	28	13	4	2	3	23	20	24	3rd
1899–1900	18	6	2	1	25	14	3	5	1	21	13	25	2nd
1900–01	20	7	1	2	25	13	6	2	2	24	15	29	2nd
1901–02	18	5	2	2	19	15	6	2	1	19	13	26	2nd
1902–03	22	4	6	1	20	15	4	4	3	16	15	26	5th
1903–04	26	11	1	1	43	12	7	1	6	25	15	38	3rd
1904–05	26	8	4	1	31	15	10	1	2	37	16	41	1st
1905–06	30	13	0	2	36	8	11	1	3	40	11	49	1st
1906–07	34	13	4	0	40	14	10	5	2	40	16	55	1st
1907–08	34	15	2	0	57	11	9	5	3	29	16	55	1st
1908–09	34	11	3	3	36	10	12	2	3	35	14	51	1st
1909–10	34	13	4	0	38	9	11	2	4	25	13	54	1st
1910–11	34	11	4	2	31	3	4	7	6	17	15	41	5th
1911–12	34	14	3	0	38	11	3	8	6	20	22	45	2nd
1912–13	34	13	2	2	32	12	9	3	5	21	16	49	2nd
1913–14	38	15	3	1	45	6	15	2	2	36	8	65	1st
1914–15	38	18	1	0	56	10	12	4	3	35	15	65	1st
1915–16	38	15	3	1	64	13	17	0	2	52	10	67	1st
1916–17	38	13	5	1	38	8	14	5	0	41	9	64	1st
1917–18	34	11	4	2	34	13	13	3	1	32	13	55	2nd
1918–19	34	13	3	1	33	10	13	3	1	38	12	58	1st
1919–20	42	15	6	0	54	14	14	4	3	35	17	68	2nd
1920–21	42	16	3	2	50	15	14	3	4	36	20	66	2nd
1921–22	42	19	2	0	51	4	8	11	2	32	16	67	1st
1922–23	38	10	5	4	29	21	9	3	7	23	18	46	3rd
1923–24	38	11	5	3	36	15	6	7	6	20	18	46	3rd
1924–25	38	13	3	3	51	13	5	5	9	26	31	44	4th
1925–26	38	15	4	0	59	15	10	4	5	38	25	58	1st

Scottish League
1926–27 to 1968–69

		Home					Away						
	P	W	D	L	F	A	W	D	L	F	A	Pts	Pos
1926–27	38	14	2	3	58	21	7	5	7	43	34	49	3rd
1927–28	38	14	3	2	56	13	9	6	4	37	26	55	2nd
1928–29	38	13	2	4	38	17	9	5	5	29	27	51	2nd
1929–30	38	12	1	6	52	21	10	4	5	36	25	49	4th
1930–31	38	16	2	1	64	14	8	8	3	37	20	58	2nd
1931–32	38	13	2	4	64	24	7	6	6	30	26	48	3rd
1932–33	38	13	3	3	47	18	7	5	7	28	26	48	4th
1933–34	38	12	5	2	47	20	6	6	7	31	33	47	3rd
1934–35	38	15	2	2	61	19	9	2	8	31	26	52	2nd
1935–36	38	17	1	1	71	16	15	1	3	44	17	66	1st
1936–37	38	14	3	2	59	26	8	5	6	30	32	52	3rd
1937–38	38	16	3	0	70	15	11	4	4	44	27	61	1st
1938–39	38	11	3	5	62	31	9	5	5	37	22	48	2nd
1939–40*	5	2	0	1	4	3	1	0	1	3	4	6	–
1946–47	30	8	2	5	30	27	5	4	6	23	28	32	7th
1947–48	30	5	4	6	21	25	5	1	9	20	31	25	12th
1948–49	30	7	3	5	26	17	5	4	6	22	23	31	6th
1949–50	30	11	4	0	37	17	3	3	9	14	33	35	5th
1950–51	30	6	3	6	29	25	6	2	7	19	21	29	7th
1951–52	30	7	5	3	30	22	3	3	9	22	33	28	9th
1952–53	30	7	3	5	33	26	4	4	7	18	28	29	8th
1953–54	30	14	1	0	40	7	6	2	7	32	22	43	1st
1954–55	30	10	4	1	42	16	9	4	2	34	21	46	2nd
1955–56	34	9	4	4	31	18	7	5	5	24	21	41	5th
1956–57	34	9	6	2	33	14	6	2	9	25	29	38	5th
1957–58	34	7	6	4	42	22	12	2	3	42	25	46	3rd
1958–59	34	11	4	2	48	24	3	4	10	22	29	36	6th
1959–60	34	7	5	5	36	24	5	4	8	37	35	33	9th
1960–61	34	9	4	4	33	22	6	5	6	31	24	39	4th
1961–62	34	12	4	1	46	16	7	4	6	35	21	46	3rd
1962–63	34	10	3	4	33	16	9	3	5	43	28	44	4th
1963–64	34	13	3	1	61	16	6	6	5	28	18	47	3rd
1964–65	34	9	2	6	33	18	7	3	7	43	39	37	8th
1965–66	34	16	1	0	66	12	11	2	4	40	18	57	1st
1966–67	34	14	2	1	61	17	12	4	1	50	16	58	1st
1967–68	34	14	3	0	53	14	16	0	1	53	10	63	1st
1968–69	34	12	3	2	50	19	11	5	1	39	13	54	1st

* *Season terminated due to the onset of the Second World War.*

Scottish League
1969–70 to 1974–75

		Home					Away						
	P	W	D	L	F	A	W	D	L	F	A	Pts	Pos
1969–70	34	12	2	3	54	18	15	1	1	42	15	57	1st
1970–71	34	15	1	1	43	7	11	5	2	46	16	56	1st
1971–72	34	15	1	1	48	14	13	3	1	48	14	60	1st
1972–73	34	14	3	0	47	10	12	2	3	46	18	57	1st
1973–74	34	12	4	1	51	12	11	3	3	31	15	53	1st
1974–75	32	11	2	4	47	20	9	3	5	34	21	45	3rd

Premier Division
1975–76 to 1996–97

		Home					Away						
	P	W	D	L	F	A	W	D	L	F	A	Pts	Pos
1975–76	36	10	5	3	35	18	11	1	6	36	24	48	2nd
1976–77	36	13	5	0	44	16	10	4	4	35	23	55	1st
1977–78	36	11	3	4	36	19	4	3	11	27	35	36	5th
1978–79	36	12	4	2	32	13	9	2	7	29	24	48	1st
1979–80	36	13	3	2	44	17	4	8	5	17	21	47	2nd
1980–81	36	12	3	3	47	18	14	1	3	37	19	56	1st
1981–82	36	12	5	1	41	16	12	2	4	38	17	55	1st
1982–83	36	12	3	3	44	18	13	2	3	46	18	55	2nd
1983–84	36	13	5	0	46	15	8	3	7	34	26	50	2nd
1984–85	36	12	3	3	43	12	10	5	3	34	18	52	2nd
1985–86	36	10	6	2	27	15	10	4	4	40	23	50	1st
1986–87	44	16	5	1	57	17	11	4	7	33	24	63	2nd
1987–88	44	16	5	1	42	11	15	5	2	37	12	72	1st
1988–89	36	13	1	4	35	18	8	3	7	31	26	46	3rd
1989–90	36	6	6	6	21	20	4	8	6	16	17	34	5th
1990–91	36	10	4	4	30	14	7	3	8	22	24	41	3rd
1991–92	44	15	3	4	47	20	11	7	4	41	22	62	3rd
1992–93	44	13	5	4	37	18	11	5	4	31	23	58	3rd
1993–94	44	8	11	3	26	21	7	9	6	25	17	50	4th
1994–95	36	6	8	4	16	14	5	10	3	23	19	51	4th
1995–96	36	12	5	1	40	12	12	6	0	34	13	83	2nd
1996–97	36	14	2	2	48	9	8	5	5	30	25	75	2nd

Did You Know That?
Celtic won more Championships in the 1970s, seven, than in any other decade.

🎉 FOR THE RECORD (cont...) 🎉

Scottish Premier League
1997–98 to 2005–06

		Home					Away					
	P	W	D	L	F	A	W	D	L	F	A	Pts	Pos
1997–98	36	12	4	2	41	9	10	4	4	23	15	74	1st
1998–99	36	14	2	2	49	12	7	6	5	35	23	71	2nd
1999–2000	36	12	3	3	58	17	9	3	6	32	21	69	2nd
2000–01	38	17	1	1	48	11	13	3	2	42	18	97	1st
2001–02	38	18	1	0	51	9	15	3	1	43	9	103	1st
2002–03	38	18	1	0	56	12	13	3	3	42	14	97	2nd
2003–04	38	15	2	2	62	15	16	3	0	43	10	98	1st
2004–05	38	15	0	4	41	15	15	2	2	44	20	92	2nd
2005–06	38	14	4	1	41	15	14	3	2	52	22	91	1st

🎉 OUR BHOYS HAVE WON THE CUP (15) 🎉

Celtic's 3–0 CIS Cup win over Dunfermline Athletic at Hampden Park on 19 March 2006 was the club's 26th League Cup final appearance[†], while Maciej Zurawski, Shaun Maloney and Dion Dublin became the 29th, 30th and the 31st players to score for Celtic in a Scottish League Cup final. The East End Park side had stifled the SPL's runaway leaders for the opening 40 minutes of the game until a blunder by the Pars' young goalkeeper, Alan McGregor, gifted the "Magic Man" himself, Maciej Zurawski, Celtic's opening goal with only two minutes of the first-half remaining. Celtic wrapped up the game in the second half with a stunning free-kick from Shaun Maloney, and their third of the game came in stoppage time when Dion Dublin, on as a substitute for his former Manchester United team-mate, Roy Keane, struck from close range to give Gordon Strachan his first trophy success as a manager.

CIS CUP FINAL 2006
19 MAY 2006, HAMPDEN PARK, GLASGOW
Celtic (1) 3   v   Dunfermline Ath (0) 0
(Zurawski 43, Maloney 77,
Dublin 90)
Att. 50,090
Celtic: Boruc, Telfer, Balde, McManus, Wallace, Nakamura,
Keane (Dublin 61), Lennon, Maloney, Zurawski, Petrov.

[†]Celtic have now won 13 League Cup finals and lost 13, scoring 56 goals and conceding 37.

❧ DARK BLUES MASSACRED ❧

Celtic inflicted Dundee's heaviest-ever defeat when they beat the Dark Blues 11–0 on 26 October 1895.

❧ MURDOCH'S WINNING RUN ❧

After going through two barren years at Celtic Park, Bobby Murdoch enjoyed a prolific run from 1965 to 1973, winning 19 major domestic medals. He won the Scottish title nine times, five Scottish Cups and five Scottish League Cups, all between 1965 and 1973.

❧ HAVE GLOVES, WILL TRAVEL ❧

Celtic goalkeeper Joe Kennaway played for Scotland against Austria in 1933, thus becoming one of a tiny number of players to represent three countries in international matches. Montreal-born Kennaway represented his native Canada and the United States of America before joining Celtic in 1931. In his eight years at Parkhead, Joe made 295 appearances for Celtic and kept 83 clean sheets.

❧ SUPER NAKA ❧

Japanese star Shunsuke Nakamura is nicknamed "Super Naka" by the Celtic fans. Nakamura's name appears as an endorsement for a football simulation game, *Winning Eleven*, in Japan and the USA.

❧ A WILY FOX ❧

On 30 January 2006, 36-year-old Dion Dublin's contract with Leicester City, nicknamed "the Foxes", was terminated by mutual consent. Within hours he had signed for Celtic. And the former England international – who can play at centre-back as well as his more regular centre-forward – did not take long to become a favourite with the fans. Less than two months after signing, Dion scored Celtic's third goal in the last minute of the CIS Cup final victory over Dunfermline Athletic at Hampden Park.

❧ POLISH TV STAR ❧

Former Celtic legend Dariusz "Jackie" Dziekanowski became a television commentator in his native Poland after he retired from playing in 1996–97.

✺ MURDOCH'S WINNING RUN ✺

After going through two barren years at Celtic Park, Bobby Murdoch enjoyed a prolific run from 1965 to 1973, winning 19 major domestic medals. He won the Scottish title nine times, five Scottish Cups and five Scottish League Cups, all between 1965 and 1973.

✺ A JOB FOR LIFE ✺

Willie Maley was the longest serving manager at Celtic. In his 43 years in charge, from 1897 to 1940, Celtic won 19 league championships, 15 Scottish Cups, 14 Glasgow Cups and 19 Glasgow Charity Cups.

✺ DALGLISH FAILS TO MAKE THE GRADE ✺

Paul Dalglish started his career as a youth team player at Celtic before joining Liverpool. However, Paul, the son of Kenny Dalglish, did not make any appearances for either of his father's clubs. On the final day of the January 2006 transfer window, former Celtic defender Tony Mowbray, manager of Hibernian, signed Paul for the Hi-Bees.

✺ RECORD SCOTTISH PREMIER LEAGUE WIN ✺

On 19 February 2006, Celtic beat Dunfermline Athletic 8–1 at East End Park to set a new Scottish Premier League record for the largest away victory. Maciej Zurawski scored four of the goals for the Bhoys.

✺ MBE FOR A BHOY ✺

In 2003, former Celtic defender Paul Elliott was awarded an MBE by the Queen in recognition of his work involving anti-racism in football.

✺ THE BHOYS ARE BACK IN TOWN (22) ✺

"I've now had the honour to stand in the middle of the pitch as manager of the champions and that was emotional. We make no claims about being a great football side, but people can't take away the fact that we are 20 points in front at the top of the league and want to get better and better. I can't believe it. As Celtic manager you can make millions of pople happy and it's a great thing to be able to do."

Gordon Strachan, on clinching the Scottish League title with a 1–0 win against Hearts on 5 April 2006

❧ THREE GOALS IN THREE MINUTES ☙

In the second leg of Celtic's 2000–01 UEFA Cup qualifying round tie against Jeunesse Esch from Luxembourg, Mark Burchill hit a hat-trick in just three first-half minutes. It helped Celtic to a 7–0 victory on the night and 11–0 on aggregate.

❧ A SMART BEAR ☙

Although John "Yogi" Hughes did not play in the 1967 European Cup Final, he was still awarded a winners' medal, having played in the requisite number of matches earlier in the competition.

❧ LARSSON'S LAST GIFT TO THE BHOYS ☙

Henrik Larsson had one final gift to Celtic, three years after leaving Celtic Park for Barcelona. In his final appearance for the Catalan club – the 2006 UEFA Champions League final against Arsenal – he came off the substitutes' bench and turned the match in Barca's favour. Larsson set up both goals as Barcelona came from 1–0 down to win 2–1. The victory affected the UEFA coefficients in such a way as to give Celtic an automatic place in the Champions League group stage for 2006–07.

❧ YOUNG BHOYS IN UEFA FINAL ☙

Not only did Celtic's under-19s complete the domestic double in their age group in 2005–06, six members of the squad helped Scotland to reach the finals of the UEFA Under-19s championship for the first time. Goalkeeper Scott Fox, defender Scott Cuthbert and midfielders Ryan Conroy, Simon Ferry, Charlie Grant and Michael McGlinchey all featured as the Scots, coached by Tommy Wilson, beat group 3 hosts Belarus and Bulgaria, as well as drawing with defending champions France, to top the group and enter the finals, held in Poland in July 2006. Grant was also named player of the tournament.

❧ THE BHOYS ARE BACK IN TOWN (23) ☙

"The best player of them all for me was Paul McStay. He was the bandleader; he conducted the orchestra. Always available to take the ball, he'd never hide; he had feet like Fred Astaire."
John Hughes, Celtic defender who joined the club in 1995, on his team-mate of the time

❧ BIBLIOGRAPHY & REFERENCES ☙

WEBSITES

www.absoluteastronomy.com ❖ www.bbc.co.uk
www.celtic.soccer24-7.com ❖ www.celticcollectorsclub.co.uk
www.celticfc.net ❖ www.celtic-mad.co.uk
www.celticprogrammesonline.com ❖ www.comeonthehoops.com
www.cowdenbeath.net ❖ www.cybertims.com
www.dailyrecord.co.uk ❖ www.eatsleepsport.com
www.eleven-a-side.com ❖ www.eleven-a-side.com
www.englandfanzine.co.uk ❖ www.englandfc.com
www.englandfootballonline.com ❖ www.eveningtimes.co.uk
www.forfarathletic-mad.co.uk ❖ www.geocities.com
www.glasgowguide.co.uk ❖ www.guardian.co.uk
www.keep-the-faith.net ❖ www.londonhearts.com
www.nafcsc.com ❖ www.napit.co.uk
www.neilbrown.newcastlefans.com ❖ www.nozdrul.plus.com
www.ntvcelticfanzine.com ❖ www.onetel.net.uk
www.psychcentral.com ❖ www.ptearlyyears.net
www.rsssf.com ❖ www.scottishleague.net
www.soccerbase.com/teams.sd ❖ www.soccerfansnetwork.com
www.sport.scotsman.com ❖ www.sporting-heroes.net
www.sundaymirror.co.uk ❖ www.uk.geocities.com
www.upyarkilt.com ❖ www.wikpedia.org
www.worldsoccer.com

SONGS

www.lyricsfreak.com
"You're In My Heart" by Rod Stewart

BOOKS

Stan: Tackling My Demons by Stan Collymore,
HarperCollinsWillow, September 2004
Honest by Ulrika Jonsson, Sidgwick and Jackson, October 2002
The Little Book of Celtic edited by Graham McCall,
Carlton Publishing Group 2004
A Scottish Football Hall of Fame by John Cairney, Mainstream, 2004

✖ INDEX ✖